The Cook's Companion

and other tasty dishes

MARGARET DUNN

Happy Home

Everyday Magic for a Colorful Life

Happy Home

Everyday Magic for a Colorful Life

Charlotte Hedeman Guéniau

Foreword by Holly Becker of Decor8

RIZZOLI
NEW YORK

New York · Paris · London · Milan

First published in the United States of America in 2013 by
Rizzoli International Publications, Inc.
300 Park Avenue South
New York, NY 10010
www.rizzoliusa.com

Originally published in the United Kingdom in 2013 by
Jacqui Small LLP
an imprint of Aurum Press Ltd
7 Greenland Street
London NW1 0ND

2013 2014 2015 2016 / 10 9 8 7 6 5 4 3 2 1

ISBN: 978-0-8478-3991-9

Library of Congress Control Number: 2012941034

Printed in China

PUBLISHER Jacqui Small
ASSOCIATE PUBLISHER Joanna Copestick
MANAGING EDITOR Lydia Halliday
PROJECT EDITOR Sian Parkhouse
ART DIRECTION & DESIGN Sarah Rock
PRODUCTION Peter Colley

J'AIME CETTE PIÈCE.

Contents

Foreword

Are you color shy? Do you dream of using more of it in your home, but haven't a clue where to begin? Perhaps you already love your colorful space, but crave new ideas and inspiration? As a design blogger, stylist, and author, I am always on the prowl for fresh ideas and *Happy Home* is jam-packed with so many creative approaches to color that you won't want to put it down! It is not only filled with whimsical homes belonging to Charlotte and her friends, but I'm certain that you'll find her encouraging, approachable, and heartfelt tone like a warm hug from a best friend. I find decorating books written in such a personal way to be so very charming, and this is precisely why *Happy Home* stands out from the pack and why you'll want to own it. It's approachable, beautiful, and positive—just like the lady who wrote it.

   I met Charlotte when I styled her home for my first book, *Decorate*, and will never forget the moment she greeted me with her warm smile, sparkling blue eyes, and colorful outfit on the front steps of her very Danish, very beautiful home. Charlotte was welcoming from the start and her energy, both positive and relaxed, extended into all that she touched, which was apparent as soon as I stepped inside and had a look around. Her love of color filled every corner, from the nearly neon pink cabinet in her workspace to the playful, blue rhino heads in the hallway and her bold, red, floral wallpaper in the kitchen. I couldn't help but smile and feel energized by the whimsy and joy that surrounded me.

   Charlotte is fearless and this quality inspires me so much. *Happy Home* will have you experimenting and feeling more bold with every flip of a new page, because her decorating confidence and no-fail approach is infectious. Her creativity, coupled with a healthy sense of humor, extends from the products that she designs for her interior collections at RICE straight into her home. Check out her entryway on page 12—how can you not fall in love at first sight with a bold canary yellow door? What about the neon pink cutlery on her living room curtains featured on pages 44 and 45? If she likes a decorating idea, then she'll simply go for it. In fact, her home is living proof that if she likes something, then that is the only validation she needs and so it stays. That's a confident decorator!

   If you're ready to have a little fun, color outside the lines, and introduce a fresh perspective to your decor, *Happy Home* with its accessible, livable, and lovable style will capture your heart from page one. When you put aside fear and just decorate, so many possibilities await. Live colorfully and happy decorating!

HOLLY BECKER founder of Decor8

Homes that make you smile

What makes a home happy? What makes a home? What makes me happy? Many thoughts have traveled through my mind during the process of writing this book. I believe it is a mixed cocktail of different ingredients. When I travel and stay in beautiful modern Zen-like hotels, I love it. But when I come home to my own house, I realize color is very much a vital ingredient in my life, a little everyday magic.

Colors, function, light, and openness are the most dominating factors in my home, and by *openness* I mean mentally as well as physically. When I go to other people's houses, the attitude of the host is what's most important to me. People who have the ability to instantly make you feel welcome, relaxed, and comfortable are always a joy to spend time with. I have felt uncomfortable in impeccable prizewinning designer homes . . . and so loved and welcome in a small and very primitive clay house in Madagascar with no toilet nearby.

I have recently moved with my husband and family to a very beautiful old house. The whole house had just been redone, but there were no colors anywhere. We came from a dream house in the country, but for practical reasons and kids' logistics, we made the "sensible" choice and moved close to schools and work. I am the kind of person who lives by my heart and my gut feeling, so this was not an easy choice. My vision was to make the house look happy, relaxed, lived in, and, of course, filled with colors. I spent lots of hours searching for wallpaper and deciding on wall colors. When the painter laid the first strokes of blue, I gave a sigh of relief. And when the first wall had wallpaper on it, I knew we would be happy there.

My hope with this book is to inspire you to make bold color choices—to stay playful with what you do in your home. Just relax—paint a single wall in a crazy color. It only takes a few hours to repaint it if you have regrets.

Sprinkle a little everyday magic throughout your home. You will be surprised by the positive impact!

CHARLOTTE HEDEMAN GUÉNIAU

clockwise from top left **BEST SEAT IN THE HOUSE** Theater seating in your own home: add crocheted throws and mismatched pillows to a rustic table, stool, and chairs to enjoy some informal downtime.

PEARLS ON A STRING These lovely rooms are bound together with a supershiny white floor and some funky rugs—an open flow of good energy. I hate closed doors and dark rooms, so I always light candles and a few lamps in the living areas. Open flow equals happy living.

LOVELY LADIES ON YOUR BED A stunning bedspread can take over a bedroom and that is quite OK—but it is better to keep walls plain-colored. I like having two or three different bedspreads to change the look of a bedroom regularly—that is really all it takes.

A HALLWAY MADE NICE You pass through it numerous times a day, so why not put a bit of thought into the things you put here—a nice rug, some pretty boxes to store all the bits and pieces, and a big, beautiful painting on the wall. An eye pleaser many times a day.

Welcome!

Just imagine if you were saying that out loud to yourself at the top of your lungs every time you opened the door to your home—WELCOME HOME! It sure would add some color to your arrival. I find the entryway such an important place. How welcome do you actually feel when you open the door? How welcome do your guests feel?

I once lived in a house with quite a big entryway with doors leading everywhere but no storage possibilities—every time I came home, I felt annoyed by the mess of shoes, bags, and clothes that would often greet me. It was a constant source of slight irritation. It was a lovely house in so many ways, but that annoyance with the hallway and the niggle of the constant clutter has stayed with me, and since then I have put a lot of effort into the entrance area of every house we have lived in.

Think about the first ten seconds you meet someone—you tune in and you get an intuitive feeling about that person. Imagine doing the same to your own entry. Imagine opening your front door—take a step back, and look with your eyes and mind completely open. Personally, I feel happy and welcome when I am greeted by just a few coats and only the necessary basics that we are using this week. Trust me, it is not always perfect—sometimes I come home and I wonder how all these jackets and coats have crept in. Why on earth do we have so many shoes? I step over a pile of schoolbags and then I am home. But I do love the days when I swing in through the door and am met by a tidy entrance with everything stored away in its rightful place.

My advice is to keep the area simple. Only have items here that you are actually using right now. Use colored storage baskets—perhaps one for each family member. Make sure you have enough hooks and hanging space for you and for guests.

Having said all this, there is of course a huge difference between how you welcome yourself to your home and how you welcome your guests. The best greeting is always a warm smile and a hug in those first ten seconds to set the scene for a sincere welcome.

A KISS, A HUG, AND A WARM WELCOME This is what greets you when you enter my house. Make sure you have enough hooks for guests—try to only keep the jackets you are using according to the season. The same goes for shoes. If you have the space, then have one basket per person to keep shoes in. I had a simple bench made so we can sit down and put on our shoes.

SUNSHINE EVERY DAY
Yellow is an all-time favorite color of mine. As a child, my room was yellow—to start with, it was my mother's choice, but now it has really become mine as well. If you believe in chakras and the healing power of colors, yellow is the color of the solar plexus, right where your gut feeling sits. A yellow door—or any color actually—is wonderful as the thing to look at before leaving your home. Follow your instinct, go with your gut, and have an awesome day.

left HOME SWEET FUNKY HOME This is a great entry, with plenty of colorful hooks and baskets and lots of drawers for gloves and scarves. A fabulous cabinet perched high on the wall can display the sexiest of your shoes.

WILLKOMMEN— BIENVENUE—WELCOME This large entrance area has a roomy closet for coats and shoes that you can choose to close off, but when you live colorfully, your clothes tend to be happy as well and deserve to be looked at. With a closet like this, it is easy to keep a tidy look. Again there is a lovely bench to sit on and put on your shoes before throwing yourself out into the real world.

Hallways and landings

Hallways are often overlooked as mere rooms to be passed through instead of places to spend time, but with a little bit of love and a few gallons of paint, you are all set. This is, after all, a passageway, and you come here many times during the day. I recently had my hall repainted, and it is amazing how much difference a new color can make. The top floor of my house has a long passageway that leads to all the bedrooms and our guest room. When we moved in, the walls were a dreary sight, and this was actually the first area I had painted. Painting the landing is a great way to brighten up an otherwise anonymous part of your home, and it instantly draws the eye upward. If you paint half-height walls, the entire entryway/landing area appears a lot more spacious than it actually is.

What happens on the floor can also help define a room. I love rugs and use them everywhere possible. They can improve the acoustic in a room by softening the sounds, which is great in a room you often step into wearing shoes. You can easily change the look of a room by changing the rugs, and there is no need to buy new ones every time you feel like changing. Just switch the rugs around. I often use them to create a connection between rooms—or simply as a splash of color on the floor. A rug at the door has many purposes. It bids you welcome, and at the same time, it wipes your feet and prevents the worst of the dirt from coming into your home. What I also love about rugs is that most of them are low-maintenance. You can easily wash or dry-clean them, and with a little effort they last you a lifetime.

opposite **HALL OF FAME** I really want to show you how much you can change the look of a room when you change the colors of the walls and pick out other decorative details. Be bold—be bright—don't be afraid. I often hear people saying "What if I get tired of it?" And I almost want to scream back: WHY oh WHY should you get more tired of a happy funky color than you get tired of a white wall? If you do get sick of a color, then you can repaint it.

above **THREE COLORS HAPPY** Bright green, strong mint, and a purple lampshade— three colors that suit each other well. I would go so far as to say they are neutral colors, not too feminine, not too masculine—just all perfect together.

right **HALLWAYS— ALWAYS** This hallway was the first room that was painted when we moved into our new home. I felt deep relief when I started seeing blue. Painting half a wall and putting up some colorful lampshades makes a difference and keeps it from getting too dark. We have a boring carpet in this hallway, partly because of the cold and partly because the floor below is not very nice. An easy way to get around this is to scatter some mats to create a nice view.

opposite **THE POWER OF PATTERN** I have a wallpaper addiction. I love how just one strip of wallpaper can change and define a whole room. It's almost magical when you put it up—it truly feels like waving a magic wand. Framing a doorway and at the same time the entrance to another room with outstanding wallpaper leaves a strong signal.

right **BELIEVE IN BLUE** In the chakras, blue is the color of the fifth chakra, the chakra for honesty or the throat chakra. So it's a great color for a hallway—get an honest welcome and speak the truth. Drenching half-height walls in summertime blue then adding in a piece of furniture in the same color creates a striking and happy effect. Finish off the color story by adding lime green vases with completely complementary yellow flowers for a breezy display that lifts the spirits. An extra idea would be to paint the wooden strip between the white and the blue in a contrast color, just for a change.

Living, loving, laughing . . .

. . . in relaxing rooms

The three words *live*, *love*, *laugh* are a cornerstone at RICE and in my own life—I actually saw the words written on a blackboard in a small café at the weekend market in Bangkok right after September 11. They just feel so right, and to me they sum up what life is all about.

I like to stand back and look at my own home from time to time as if it were the first time I saw it, especially the living room. The description says it all—it is a room to live your life in, doing all the things that makes you really happy and comfortable.

Simply try to look at it with an outsider's eye—does this space make me feel happy, content? Is there anything bothering my eye? Does it match up to where my life is at the moment?

When my children were little, we had a big couch standing in front of a window. The children and their friends loved jumping from the windowsill onto the couch—again and again and again, for hours on end! Needless to say we do not have this couch anymore, but it was great fun while it lasted. In this period of our lives, when the kids were small, that is, lots and lots of open floor space was my priority.

We had lots of mattresses we could all lie on and play, read books, or just cuddle. There was even room enough to roam around on a tricycle. We had tough floors to withstand the wear and tear and left enough space for routes in and among the furniture.

As your life moves, on your needs change. That's why it's important to take stock every now and then. Sometimes moving house forces you to refocus, but if you stay in the same home, it's important to make sure it still works well for you. Does your home allow you to be the person you want to be and give space for your family? Does it stimulate and refresh, nurture and nourish you? There are always elements we can look at and fix, but if you harbor the feeling of having found a basically good spot to live, love, and laugh in, then you can never go wrong.

previous pages **BRIGHT AND INVITING** This is a light, feminine space where you can ask friends for high tea or just hang out by yourself. Pale colors and different textures make a cozy and restful combination.

far left **ROOMS WITH A VIEW** I love painted wooden floors—it is like dancing on cream, both for your eyes and your feet. If you have several rooms adjoining, they connect really well if the floors are all white and scattered with colorful rugs in mixed materials for a fun look and feel.

left **TAKE A SEAT** Having small sitting areas around the house is very inviting. To sometimes change your habits and just have a cup of tea with a friend in a spot where you do not normally sit might even lift conversations to new levels. To draw you in, introduce some pattern on textiles or in the form of wallpaper and interesting artwork on the walls.

GLORIOUS MIX Keeping a white base on the walls is always the safe choice in a room—it leaves an open playground for colors on paintings, pillows, and carpets. Make sure you add textures in pillows, rugs, and furniture. Combining simple appliqué and floral prints in mixy-matchy tones gives a cozy feeling.

"Your living room should cater to you and your needs. If you love having friends over, make sure that there are enough comfortable seats. If you like to hang out by yourself, you need a different setup. Decorate it so it emphasizes your personality to the max."

Smiling spaces

Mother Teresa said, "Every time you smile at someone, it is an action of love, a gift to that person, a beautiful thing." A smile is contagious and such a simple thing to do. Create spaces that put a smile on your face or send you a happy smile when you walk in and your guests, too, will notice and remember. Why not live in a home that provides that feeling all the time?

Who does not wish to be remembered in connection with a happy smiling feeling? When people come to my own home or to visit our office or showrooms, we almost always get the comments "You can't help smiling when you enter this place" or "Wow—it makes me happy inside just to be here." I truly believe colors can do that— make you smile from deep within.

But other things can put a smile on your face as well—the small kitschy souvenirs you have bought, the odd gift with quirky appeal, the beautiful heirloom pieces and things with a personal story behind them that mean something to you all give you that smiley feeling. I love to have a mix of heirlooms, clay figures given to me by my children, plastic-fantastic figurines, and exquisitely handmade boxes and jars within eyesight. If you have a more traditional approach to decorating, one or two items will be fine to start with—you can always add more. When arranged in little tableaux or just placed singly around your house, they quickly become eye-catching attention seekers. You can use this to your advantage. If there's a corner, a piece of furniture, or a windowsill you wish to enhance, place a little happy-feeling smile breaker at that spot. It will divert attention from other areas, which might be a good thing sometimes. But do not overflow every surface with funny things— keep them carefully gathered in thoughtfully selected spots.

opposite, left KITSCH AND THAT Look for a variety of items that look funky together, and in between place a few functional items such as candleholders and a vase. Then build up around that with some kitschy or crazy items that will make you smile.

opposite, right FUNKY LINEUP If you enjoy collecting, it is a good idea to line a few items up next to one another and then add a small showstopper—something that surprises your eye and makes you twitch a smile.

right LADIES LOUNGING Some spaces are allowed to be ultrafeminine—there have been so many cigar-filled gentlemen's clubs over the years, I like the idea of a ladies' lounge. Choose a romantic wallpaper but with a humorous twist. Make sure there are pillows enough to throw yourself down with a good book. Invite a few ladies over for tea and a chat. Choose a quirky mix of art and pictures of different styles to hang on the wall to avoid too serious a look.

MIRROR MIRROR ON THE WALL Mirrors are a great space enlarger I like to have in my house. If you cannot find an antique mirror, you can search for an old large frame from a painting you don't especially like and then get a mirror placed inside. Using fun graphic prints on pillows or walls casts a quirky reflection in this room.

RAISE A SMILE TO LIGHT UP YOUR HOME

Who doesn't like to feel cheerful? Little funny displays throughout your home will bring a smile on your face, show off beloved pieces, or just draw the eyes to a certain point.

✻ **Gather a small collection** of funny, kitschy, and stylish items, and arrange them where they can be seen every day.

✻ **Create a set piece** with art on the wall and a little table below with vases, lanterns, or other things to accentuate it.

✻ **A neon-colored piece** of furniture will highlight a quiet corner.

✻ **Animals always inspire** affection, so include them as prints on fabrics, as small ornaments, or even as a brightly colored papier-mâché deer's head on the wall.

✻ **Display a personal collection** of everyday items in colorful combinations to give youself a warm feeling.

✻ **Flowers will always lift** the atmosphere, even in the darkest corner. I'm never without them in my home.

✻ **If you leave a painting** standing on the table, it is easy to change out and replace with something else whenever you feel like it.

right **CORNERED** Place a small table in a corner and add some lighting to draw the attention—after that, you can play with different kinds of small exhibitions that you change regularly, like these happy mixes of artwork and objects.

left **WALLS OF FAME** A wall is like an empty playground—just use your imagination and let the games begin. If you choose a wallpaper with lots of prints like this one, there is no need for a single nail. If you use lots of frames, scraps, bits, and pieces and place them in a pattern, you can create the same effect.

opposite **ARRESTING ARTWORK** One single painting is enough sometimes to dress a big wall, and if you have lots of pillows to throw around you are good to go. Add zesty color with bright textured pillows and statement pieces of art on the walls. Elsewhere, keep walls and floors plain and simple so the art and the textiles do most of the visual talking.

Have fun with your walls

A wall is like a blank canvas—so full of opportunities. Colorful paint? Funky wallpaper? Or a pristine white wall that leaves the world wide open for you to play with frames, photos, and pictures? I like to put a lot of old plates on a wall, mixing them with photos, paintings, and lithography. Or sometimes I even put up sticks in the shape of letters using masking tape—see page 32 if you want to try this. It is really only your own imagination that sets the limit.

The paintings I have seem to have just come to me. I never consciously went out and said I need something for this wall in this or that color scheme. It has been more of a true-love-at-first-sight-struck-by-lightning kind of feeling when I have bought the paintings we have—and by some kind of magic, there has always been exactly the right empty wall ready in welcome.

If you paint a wall in a room, it changes the feeling and the look completely. Actually it only takes a few hours to do this, and a bucket of paint is not much more expensive than a good bottle of wine. I mostly choose to paint only one wall in a room in a bright color—I find it more soothing, as a fully painted room can seem overwhelming.

Then there's wallpaper, another passion of mine. I can spend hours searching on the Internet for wallpaper—there are so many fabulous wallpapers around, both in old vintage prints and brand-new ones.

Play with fabric

Using textiles to change the look of your home is probably the fastest way to do a makeover. If you change the pillows or buy a new blanket, it gives new energy to a space and gives you almost the same happy feeling as when you have bought a nice new dress. (I said almost!)

Few of us change furniture several times a year—there are pieces of furniture that live with you for years and other pieces that are part of your family heritage and you

above **FIDDLING WITH FABRIC** I love changing my blankets and pillows a few times during the year—like changing from a summer to winter wardrobe. The look of a room can change completely when you do this and keep your home feeling fresh.

stick together for better or worse till death do you part. If you have an old sofa that you are really fed up with, just use a few blankets to cover it up and add some pillows to it—it is soft, cozy, and comfortable, and suddenly you can fall in love again with your old, boring sofa.

I always keep stacks of blankets everywhere in the house—I love to cuddle up in a blanket when having a cup of tea or watching a good movie. It is so comforting. Even in my car we have pillows and a blanket. In my world, blankets must be soft, colorful, and washable—the essence of fun and function—and there should only be enough pillows on a couch that you can still sit there and feel comfortable. A pillow should not be there for the look alone but to make you feel cozy and well.

left **LIPSTICK FOR YOUR COUCH** An old, tired sofa can shine in a few new quilts and blankets packed neatly around the seats and back—like a woman feels a lot better with refreshed makeup.

"Pillows and throws provide instant warmth and comfort in a cozy space. Make sure you combine fun crochet with luxurious wool and bright patterns with subtle solids for a perfect mix of inviting textiles to keep you snuggled up and smiling."

TEXTILES TALK Zesty colors in appliqué designs on a quiet gray couch set a good calm scene—classic but absolutely *not* boring.

above **QUILT LOVE** In an all-white space, a reupholstered Gustavian-style sofa in soft gray-green checks is softened with pillows and a quilt. I love throwing quilts everywhere—even in my car. It is so comforting to roll up in a nice blanket. I always go for washable quilts so they are easy to throw in the machine.

opposite MAKING PICTURES WITH PATTERN
When you keep to very straight lines in pillows and wall decorations, you get a very organized, more formal look. If you choose a subtle base color, you obtain a more masculine look. I have a foible for work made by hand—hand-embroidered pillows amaze me every time I look at one. Respect to the people who are so skilled.

right **ANIMAL HOUSE**
The detail in this intricate owl picture is so beautiful, even the giraffe can't help but be impressed! All the textiles add something to the overall picture, even the multistriped lamp shade.

"Add zesty color with bright textured pillows and statement pieces of art on the walls. Elsewhere, keep walls and floors plain and simple so the art and the textiles do most of the visual talking."

HAPPY HOME MAKE

words of wonder

I have a serious crush on washi tape and its endless possibilities. It's Japanese masking tape that comes in so many different colors and designs. There are lots of online sites that sell it, and you can't help but be creative with it.

Look for branches in the shape of letters when you go for a walk in the woods—or maybe stones, leaves, or feathers. Stick them to the wall in the nicest messages. You can use washi tape to make a personalized door sign if you live in an apartment—or as door signs for the kids' rooms.

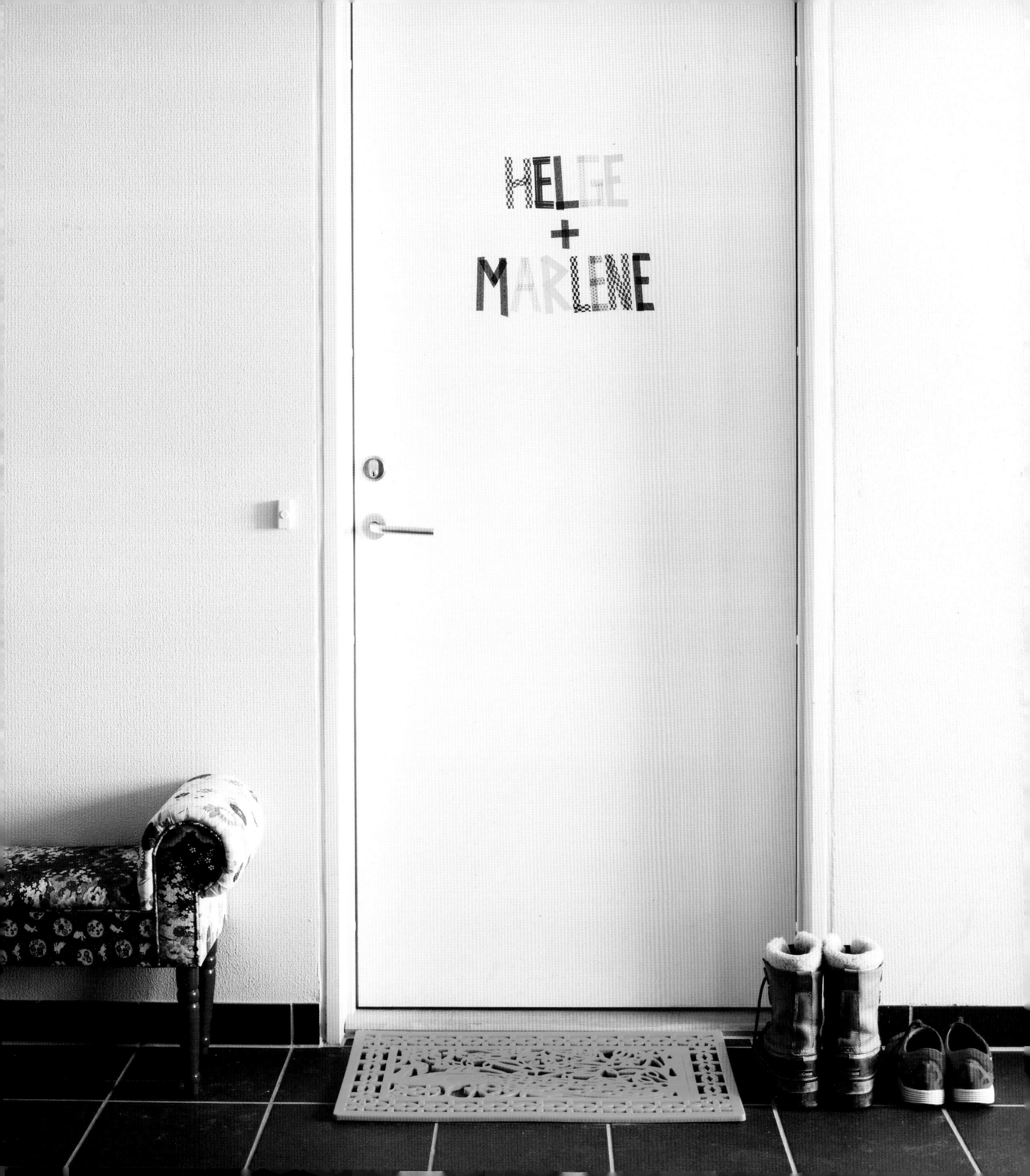
HELGE
+
MARLENE

Mixy matchy

A neon-colored flower-printed skirt worn with a blue and white T-shirt will rock my world and put a smile on my face. Try it! Follow your instinct and step out of your comfort zone and do something crazy just for the fun of it. I love the mix of old furniture and family heirlooms with modern funky and humorous items.

How to give a recipe for mixing and matching in your living room? I suppose for me, the easiest way to explain it is with reference to cooking, as that is my great love and passion. I met my husband when aged only eighteen in Paris, where we lived for fifteen years, and I was by no means a master chef, but being married to a French guy, you are bound to improve. Over time, I developed a confidence in cooking—trying ingredients, matching tastes, textures, colors, and experimenting. Following my intuition, going to the local food markets, and just letting my eyes, ears, and nose guide me was pure meditation for my mind. I would end up buying too much and often had to invite friends for dinner.

In the same way I experiment with and explore food, I like to live with colors and lots of different stuff for the home. I mix and match and mix and don't match. I follow my instinct and I am not scared to try something new and crazy. I move stuff around—sometimes it works and if not, I just change it again. I try to stay playful—a small, everyday magic moment for me can be looking at an avocado and a lemon curling up on a printed plate, perhaps with pink flamingos all over. I have inherited a beautiful chest of drawers from my grandmother. I know she would find my way of styling it a bit much, but I enjoy placing modern, quirky items on it, and every time I open a drawer, I can still feel her and almost smell her.

opposite, left **MIXING OLD AND NEW** Functional and decorative items with candles and a lamp work well in their own small universe on a defined surface.

opposite, right **FAMILY HEIRLOOMS ARE HERE TO STAY** If you are lucky enough to have some, make the best of it. The challenge is keeping them up to date. My advice is to mix in some colorful items and personal bits and pieces, such as paintings to tell the story of today.

right **CLASSIC MEETS CONTEMPORARY** This beautiful Louis XVI chest of drawers is a family inheritance from my beloved grandmother. She always had gold-plated candleholders and an antique mirror above it. I need to give it a less matching look to fit it into my world. I am certain she would not be too impressed.

left FUNK IT UP, BABY
Using a few black stylish pieces frames a colorful world in a very nice way, while the oversize Anglepoise floor light messes with our sense of scale. The rug is amazing—a riot of brightly colored bobbles. If at all possible, leave space to be playful—leaving a Hula-Hoop in your living room might incite you to turn up the volume and shake your body for ten minutes while somebody else is doing the cooking.

opposite FORMALLY INFORMAL A classically styled lamp shade and base sit happily next to a comfortable cane chair. Black is a smart color to use for definition. The cabinet could be seen as serious but is filled with interesting things and topped with swirly vases to add height and movement. The high chairs create a natural partition in the room, giving this little corner an ounce of privacy.

"The straight and strict lines of the cupboard get interesting counterplay from the curvy lines of the chair, softening the seriousness. Using the same color but different materials gives things a subtle twist."

left **PAST PERFECT**
Mixing French furniture and rattan chairs could become quite old-fashioned and classic as a look, but when you add colorful pillows with embroidery and funky details plus a modern lamp, you build a nice bridge into the fusion of old and new.

opposite **ROCK MY WORLD** A rocking chair has something therapeutic about it. I'm not sure what it is, but it does work wonders. It brings the child out in even the most serious people and the feel of a plantation porch to this romantic corner. The bright swirl of the patchwork stops it tipping over into becoming precious.

CLEVER COMBINATIONS

A mix of old and new can create a very personal touch in any room. Go for the fun and unexpected item to send things a little off balance. Don't banish family heirlooms to dusty corners or hide them in the spare room. Celebrate them and make them part of your home.

✳ **If you have an old piece** of furniture, place some quirky funky items on it so it does not look too classic and old-fashioned—and vice versa on a very modern piece of furniture.

✳ **Mix materials** to keep things interesting. Use wood, plastic, ceramic, glass—everything.

✳ **Pick your favorite items** and group them in little displays that tell a story.

✳ **Choose one dominant** piece of furniture per room and let that take center stage.

✳ **Step back and take a look.** Is what you see pleasing to your eye? Does it give you that happy feeling? Then you've got it right.

✳ **Don't think you have to fill** the whole room with this style, or it can feel a little hectic. Mixy matchy is best enjoyed in parts of a room or selected areas rather than en masse.

✳ **Provide unexpected elements** such as oversize lamp shades, homely rugs, or faux antlers. They make for visual interest and always become a conversation piece.

✳ **Create the feel of a rural homestead** by adding crocheted throws and patterned pillows to a rustic table, bench, and chairs for some mismatched comfort.

Fun and quirky things I love

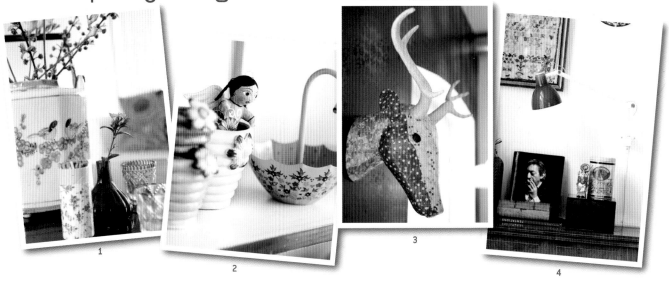

1

2

3

4

1. Cherry blossoms never fail to raise a smile. Real blossom sprigs arranged in vases, sprigs painted on tins, and cherry blossom colors sing a song of spring always. 2. Expose your small pots and bowls neatly next to each other while they are waiting patiently to be used again—throw in an unexpected little angel or funky item just to surprise the curious eyes. 3. Humor is key. This jolly reindeer in papier-mâché looks like he knows what the day has in store. 4. However politically incorrect, cigars are a good ingredient for a special evening. In our home, they only come out when the atmosphere is particularly joyful.

1

2

3

4

1. Search out a quirky object and place it next to favorite pieces such as a vase or personal treasures. 2. Vintage tins are endlessly fascinating as blasts from the past and form delightful still-life vignettes when displayed alongside old children's shoes, vintage books, and colorful papers. 3. Pressed-glass dishes and perfume bottles lined up together against old photographs are vintage classics. 4. I love old plates—these flea-market treasures become so much more special if you hang them on a wall either singly or in mismatched groups.

Opposite, clockwise from top left: Colorful and shimmering—small glass vases are simple but dramatic displays. With just a tiny flower in each, you are good to go; You can use scraps of wallpaper for gift wrapping or to line shelves once you have used them on your walls; The power of flowers—on print, metal, for real, it seems one can never get too much; Be nice to yourself—when you make tea or coffee, prepare a beautiful tray. Put a napkin or a small vase with a flower on your tray—make it a visual feast as well.

Glamourama

I love this word—I spotted it on a "beauty salon" in New Delhi in a very poor area: Ladies Salon For Glamourama. We can all do with a bit of glamour in our lives—I will always advocate fun and playfulness, but we can enjoy our more grown-up, sophisticated selves as well.

My grandmother was a stylish lady, never a hair out of place and always with immaculate nails. The small two-bedroom apartment where she spent her last years actually felt like a castle. You were not allowed to jump on the couches in her house, but she really knew how to coordinate shapes and colors. And she had this old cupboard she called the "show off" cupboard—she displayed beautiful treasures in it, and each had a story to tell. She always placed them so they would look their best and bring out the beauty in the surrounding items. When she hosted a dinner party she would make sure never to serve food in only the same colors. If you served white asparagus as a starter, there was no way you could serve white fish as a main course. Hostess with the mostest indeed!

I love going to places where you can look into the "show off" cupboard to see the history of a family—the mix of new, colorful ceramics and a few pieces from auntie's old dinner set, and perhaps a small, kitschy, glittery treasure that you found at a flea market somewhere. Your own glamourama look might be a bit more thought through and deliberate than mixy matchy, with a more stylish and luxurious line through everything. This does not mean that quirky is not welcome, but the quirkiness tends to come from more high-end purchases rather than flea-market finds. Pieces like that often need a little more space and clean-cut surroundings in order to stand out to their full advantage. When you have spent quite a bit on a piece. you do not want it to blend into the surroundings, becoming invisible. So be careful not to cram too much together; keep it tidy and on the simple side. A single vase or two, for example, will be enough to create a glamorous look for your coffee table.

Think about the overall lines in the room—arrange your decorative pieces so they accentuate the paintings or bring out the lines in a contemporary piece of furniture.

opposite STAY GLAM AND ROCK ON Think of your displays as a catwalk. Mix in a few good items--make sure they are different in color and material—and keep it simple. These white cube cupboards can be used to store different pieces so you can rotate what you put on display.

right GLAZED OVER I love a cabinet with glass doors—it is a real magnet for curious people like myself. However, you must keep it simple, airy, and organized inside; otherwise, it starts to look cluttered and loses its appeal.

SERENE STYLING My home is an open home—we always have room for a few extra people. If you like this kind of lifestyle, make it easy for people to hang out by selecting the right pieces—easy for them to pull over a small table, easy to sit close enough to be able to have real eye contact. If you set this kind of scene, the rest will follow.

Showing off

If you've got it, flaunt it! It's fun to use that beautiful wooden box you inherited or the silver teapot that was your grandmother's pride and joy—even if she only brought it out a few times a year, isn't it so much better to use it every day and not save it for that special big moment? It will bring so much more pleasure that way and give you that feeling of being spoiled every day. I love mixing old favorites with more kitschy-looking items—I enjoy the twinkle it gives when prized items of one century kiss kitschy, glittery things from this decade.

Don't save it for a rainy day. The chances of you using the things you put out in the open are much higher than if you choose to place them at the back of a dark cupboard. You really want to avoid a dusty museum kind of look and a messy mix of just anything, so keep it simple and tight-looking at all times. Less is more—even when it comes to showing off. Putting your minibar on a few trays in your living room might remind you from time to time to sit down and have a good old-fashioned drink. You can use the time to consider if you are on the right track.

below **COMFORT AND JOY** This couch screams *welcome . . . settle in . . . hang out . . . just be*. It fits the room perfectly. Building a shelf behind the sofa is a good way of making room for a display area for books and artwork. This gives an airy feeling instead of being squashed against a wall. A touch of silk on the walls and a shag-pile rug add to the luxury.

opposite **GLAMOROUS GALLERY** A built-in shelf gives possibilities for displaying and for keeping things you like to use regularly nearby—your favorite books, some nice baskets to store your knitting gear. Keep it simple—when using the same shape of basket in different colors, you create a nice color palette and at the same time a calm, organized overview.

GET SOME GLAMOUR IN YOUR LIFE

I have a few objects that always feel very glamorous to me—glamorous because of their look or their function, such as a treasured art deco bottle opener. It's about combining the contemporary pieces with just enough classical styling here and there to demonstrate confidence and calm.

✳ **Lavish fabrics** such as silk and velvet can add a lot of glamour to even the most eclectic room, creating a sense of indulgence.

✳ **Your grandmother's antique** chest of drawers adds a more adult touch to your home and allows you to play with the funky little touches around it.

✳ **Well-designed furniture,** such as solidly built sofas and organic kidney shapes for retro small tables, adds flair with functionality.

✳ **Understated shine** in the form of a striped silk wallpaper on one wall will lift a room.

✳ **Create a focal point** with your lighting by installing a period-piece chandelier, and work the rest of the room around it.

✳ **Metallic elements** in the form of candlesticks, lamp bases, or small figures and statues add a hint of richness.

✳ **Allow plenty of space** for your displays to breathe—this suggests a degree of consideration and measured thought.

✳ **Layering luxury textures** and materials suggests richness and interest. Think wool, silk, leather, and polished wood.

above **SHAPE AND FORM** The very straight and strict lines in the sofa and the wall art are softened by the organic table and the flowing lines in the lamp. The color theme works its way through everything from the painting to the pillows and even the books, creating a gathered, thought-through feeling.

left **CALM COLORS** The palette is subtle, but different prints and textures inspire.

opposite **AN EYE FOR STYLE** This room has clearly been decorated with careful thought and consideration. The mix of styles works well due to the very organized way everything is displayed, but there are still lots of interesting splashes to keep your attention.

"A sense of calm envelops this cool living room where comfortable furniture and contemporary lines contribute to a relaxed and comfortable space in which to hang loose with friends and family."

Glamorous things I love

1. An unusually shaped statue/candleholder—I love when an item surprises you. *2.* A decorative souvenir from good times spent adds a layer of another country's style in your home. *3.* Make a virtue of showing family heirlooms, but mix the classical with a colorful basket so your home does not look like a shrine or a museum. *4.* Darker pieces have a solidity that will ground a room as they draw the eye downward. Candles add instant glamour wherever you place them.

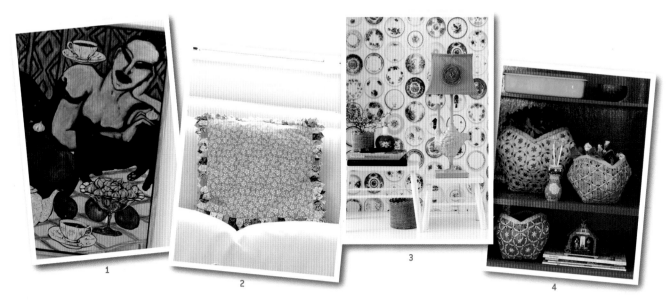

1. Art with food—the colors' motives, to me, are very sensual and life-invigorating, and eating well and with friends is part of everyday magic. *2.* Extra detailing on a simple pillow, always special to look at. *3.* Mixing a small world of quirky items backed by a beautiful wallpaper is visually enjoyable, and if at the same time you include nice lighting and a candleholder, you are all set for a good atmosphere. *4.* Displaying your knitwear in progress in colorful baskets makes it nice to look at and perhaps helps remind you to keep working on it.

Opposite, clockwise from top left: A rhino as a flowerpot, the ultimate happy marriage of grown-up humor and styling. Be bold in your color choices. If you place colors together with dark wood, it makes for a good balance as well; Mixing patterns, shapes, and boxes within the same color tones ensures that in spite of the mixy matchy, you get a calm yet funky expression; Be brave when you choose colors for your lamp shades—classic shapes in good color combinations lift them out of the ordinary; Museum display cases and quirky oddments suggest a well-traveled life.

Glorious color

When my daughter was very young, she would often ask me, "What is your favorite color this week?" My favorite color does change according to the season and according to my mood, and it is perhaps also influenced by the colors used in the fashion industry.

There is usually always some shade of pink involved in my top five colors. It's sometimes a soft, romantic shade and at the moment a more hysterical energetic fluorescent tone of neon. Different shades of neon colors, I think, brighten up the most neutral of homes—even beige can become funky with a splash of neon orange. This newfound neon love started in India a few years back. My friend and I were traveling there for work, and we kept seeing these amazingly dressed women and men in the most wonderfully matching fluorescent clothing. It became a sport spotting them and taking pictures of them. A lot of the RICE collection is based around color and we take inspiration from the colors we find on our regular travels to India and the Far East. They are surprisingly easy to work with once you get used to allowing a little color in your life.

Fluorescent colors are not easily available—you get them on paper print, perhaps, or on certain fabrics, but to find wall paint or any kind of kitchen- or tableware in neon is a challenge. Perhaps it is just as well—I think an entire wall in neon would be a bit too much, even for me. But as a small splash thrown in here and there, it is wonderful and very uplifting. I love to spray a branch in a bright neon color and just place it in a vase, then use it as a Christmas decoration or hang it from the ceiling. Neon colors are often available in spray cans, so you can fool around and perhaps spray some of your old garden pots or your sticky-tape dispenser.

Why do so many household appliances only come in the most boring colors? A plain white iron, for example—why not a polka-dotted one? You may as well enjoy looking at something cute when you have to iron. It's the same story with the vacuum cleaner—when you must take it for a spin, why not have a fuchsia and yellow version to make the chore less boring? Give me more color? Yes, please, anytime and every day.

opposite, left A NEW DRESS, PLEASE If you have a simple vase you would like to funk up, you can wrap it in different fabric scraps and attach a small piece of embroidery or a little plastic flower.

opposite, center TWO TONES WORK WONDERS If you fix a panel of wood on a plain wall and paint the bottom of the wall in a dark color, you get a very different look. You can even use the wooden panel to support some decorative hooks.

opposite, right CROSSING OVER If you find some old flea-market embroideries or if you are lucky enough to have inherited some, use them, frame them, live with them—they suit kitschy plastic very well.

right LET'S GET IT STRAIGHT If you have straight lines as a base, you can go crazy with glorious and glamorous colors—the lines will help keep a calm base in spite of the explosion of happy colors.

Color me happy

Perhaps we should start a movement in support of color. Color me happy—wouldn't that be fun? Cars would be so much more fun if they had a lot more color on the inside and on the outside. Whoever decided that only different shades of black, gray, and beige were to be used inside almost every car? And if you want to resell a car, black is the safe color. But why?

Colored walls are one of my darlings. Just one wall can really make a huge difference in a room. I always say just do it. Give it a try. Do not worry, do not take it so seriously—it is just a wall! I often hear people talking about wanting to paint a wall in a new color, discussing, worrying—will we get sick of it? If you do get sick of it, all it takes is a bucket of paint and a couple of hours, and you can just change it back. This is so much easier than changing your husband, partner, or child. Imagine if we were just as hesitant in these matters. Oh, no, I am afraid to marry him, I might get sick of it. Nothing much would happen then. . . .

right **LIVE LIFE TO THE MAX** Yes, yes, yes is the feeling of this living room. Straight, classic lines are the base, shaped by the simple sharp lines of the couch. Play with textures and colors everywhere else. One large painting picks up a few of the colors in the pillows. If you needed a change, you could just repaint the purple walls, perhaps in a soft mint color, and with just a few hours of painting, you would feel like you had a new living room. It really does not take much effort to make major visual changes.

HANDLING COLOR WITH CONFIDENCE

There are lots of ways of introducing strong colors in your home. Jolly up small spaces by making a feature of walls and accessories. When it comes to creating colorful rooms, go with your heart and use colors you love.

✳ **Fluorescent colors** work best as details in a quiet environment. If you live in an all-white world, neon is cool. If you live in a black-and-white world, it is totally awesome.

✳ **A spray-painted branch** in a vase is a great eye-catching detail.

✳ **Paint or wallpaper** on one wall is often enough—if not, then on two opposite walls.

✳ **If all the walls are painted** in a dark color, the room will appear smaller.

✳ **If you have wooden floors,** paint them white to lift and brighten the room. This creates a great playground and a quiet base for everything else.

✳ **Don't be afraid to mix colors,** but very vivid shades can quickly become overwhelming. Stick to one or two bright colors, and add to them with softer shades.

✳ **Vases and jugs and other ceramics** can tip your color palette in one direction or another. Make a mix using a variety of bold shades of vases, pitchers, and containers, or gather together an array of softer colors.

✳ **Try an arrangement** of containers in a single color for a themed statement.

✳ **Keeping the accessories** in just a few colors creates a calming ambience.

above **NO-HOLDS-BARRED** When it comes to bringing in color, only your imagination is the limit. Use an old ice bucket as a flowerpot—mix it with a handpainted wooden box and a nice lantern. Be bold and brave.

left **HOT SHOT** Place a fluorescent item as a contrast to white for a real wow factor.

opposite **SOFAS TO SINK INTO** When I found these deeply toned mega chairs, it was love at first sight. When I lie in them I feel like I am getting a huge hug. Comfort is the key—soft, cozy, and good-looking are extra benefits. A nice blanket and someone to cuddle with—when I am lucky, two children and a dog—and I am happy.

"This room is flooded in sunlight for a large part of the day, so I opted for cool and calm colors. Mint on the walls is teamed with dark purple sofas. White for the doors, window frames, and curtains keeps the impression of the room light and airy despite the dark furniture."

HAPPY HOME MAKES

dress me up, please

An easy way to give new life to an old stool is to paint the woodwork. For an extra face-lift, sew a cover out of fabric scraps or old vintage handkerchiefs. Gather it all together underneath with elastic using the same principle as a shower cap.

Ribbons and crocheted details finish things off nicely. Mixed together with a contrast-colored fabric, they can also cover up any rough edges. The ribbon can be glued firmly in place with fabric glue.

shady ladies

If you feel like being creative, an easy project is decorating a simple white lamp shade using paper or fabric scraps.

Cut small half circles, and make a scalloped edge by gluing the circles to the bottom edge of the shade. Buy some velvet ribbon, and make a lovely finishing contrast touch at the top of the shade. Or use pieces of paper to make a flower or form a pattern— just glue them onto a solid-colored shade. Good-looking results without much effort.

WHAT A SHOWSTOPPER
Get a good carpenter
to make you built-in
seating using medium-
density fiberboard
(MDF), leaving room for
storage underneath—
fun and function in
one fell swoop. Buy
custom-size foam
mattresses for seats,
and then you can play
with different quilts
and pillows and very
easily change the
whole look in your
living room.

"There are so many bright saturated colors in this mix, this room really zings. When using so many strong colors, it is best to keep the walls white so the colors stay true and clean."

Cozy corners

Where is the center of gravity in your home when you have friends over? When you hang out with the family? And where is your own private cozy corner, where you can enjoy a cup of tea or coffee, sit with your laptop, read a book, or meditate and stare out of the window or just into the blue?

Think about that special place where you can relax and recharge your batteries. Hopefully, it does not take long to say where this particular spot is in your home. You should immediately be able to mentally connect to this place. Some would say "in front of my TV," but that is another kind of relaxation spot. What we are really looking for is a quiet spot with no noise, simply you and some beautiful accessories, with a few shots of color to make you feel good.

If you do not have a place like this in your home, I advise you to create one as soon as possible. You do not need much—a comfy chair or some big pillows, some light coming in. Then bring in the things that make you happy. The important thing is that it is a spot that feels peaceful to you, where you can recharge. My cozy corner is the best place for me to enjoy some quiet time, and I wouldn't miss it for the world.

We asked each person who participated in this book to make a beautiful tray to bring to their cozy corner. It is so nice to look after yourself in that way—a small tray with tea or coffee, perhaps some fresh fruit or a little cake and a mini vase with a colorful flower in it. The little things like this make a huge difference—everyday magic on a tray.

left **TEATIME TREAT** I have a thing for trays. It is really an everyday magic moment for me when I gather cups and plates on a tray mixed together in a happy union—my heart smiles with me.

below left **FOOD FOR THOUGHT** Never underestimate the power of visual joy. When you eat and drink food or snacks served on a beautiful plate or tray, it lifts the experience from the ordinary to the special. Focusing on what you are eating and also how you serve it, it makes a difference.

opposite **MY FEEL-GOOD CORNER** We have had these two raspberry-colored chairs for a long time, but they were placed in the wrong spot in our old house, and no one ever sat in them. Since we have moved, they are just in the right place, and this chair has become my special spot. I sit here when I am home alone, with a drink, a cup of tea, or a book. My husband has "his" chair opposite, and when we have no guests or kids around, this is where we meet. If you have a great chair but never sit in it, try to find a new spot for it in your house—it might change the way you use it.

"There is nothing quite like the happiness you get from sitting down on some furniture you love, in a room you've thought about and styled over time to simply relax, talk, or think. Indulge yourself from time to time, and simply just be in your space."

"Making a quiet space, whether it's in the corner of a room or in a small space on its own, will give you somewhere to take time out after a busy day or allow you some creative thinking space or a private place in which to read or sew."

left **FLOWER POWER**
Having your favorite spot in your home is so important, a private retreat where you feel connected to yourself, able to focus on reading, having a cup of tea—breathing all the way. If you do not have a corner like that, I highly recommend you make room for one. Today is better than tomorrow.

opposite **LIKE A CAT IN THE SUN** Daylight and a ray of sunshine works wonders for a cozy corner. Neon colors are hot—throw them in as a splash where you can, to give yourself a serious mental vitamin boost.

Colorful things I love

1

2

3

4

1. Raffia—the gold of Madagascar. I love this natural material and its many virtues. Baskets from Madagascar were the real start to our company, so they hold a special place in my heart. I love carrying my world around in a colorful bag. *2.* ROAR—a green dinosaur attacking your flowers is a fun and fabulous little detail on a table. *3.* Mixing material, items, and the kids' art from school—all chosen for their colors. *4.* Using books to create height on which to place a small object is a great idea and allows you to really appreciate the blue on this enameled candlestick.

1

2

3

4

1. Pillows—the easiest and cheapest way to give your couch a color makeover is new pillow covers. Mix not match, but always think cuddly comfort before anything else. *2.* Creating different heights either with books or a small box as a podium when you place flowers or pots in a window makes for a more interesting look. *3.* A beautiful tea cozy made by my grandmother—I love it and think of her every time I use it. This embroidery and the color mix could inspire some future prints. *4.* My favorite gift for my thirtieth birthday, a pink rhino lamp—the essence of humor, color, and function for me.

Opposite, clockwise from top left: Glitter, glamour, glass, neon, and a little Ganesh—Hindu god and lord of success and preventer of evil. Happiness in a few square inches; Nobody does it better than Mother Nature—my favorite flowers are the ones that look like you just picked them in a garden or a field; Yum yum—a feast for the eyes and the body, in my opinion; Orange and bubblegum pink really suit each other—a happy, long-lasting marriage.

Cooking, eating, sharing . . .

. . . in colorful kitchens

In my world, cooking, and food itself, is so very important, essential even—it may sound strangely superficial to some, but to me it makes a lot of sense. Food really can lift my spirit. Cooking can be meditational to me, and sharing moments of food made with love is what life is all about.

Recently we had some friends over for an improvised dinner—the kind of dinner I love. My friend quickly ran home and picked up a few things from her fridge, and I started cooking with her fifteen-year-old son. He asked me when and how I learned to cook—and it got me thinking. I really do not know how and when exactly I got going. I grew up in a family where cooking was considered easy—my mother was never stressed about having lots of guests over, and my grandmother also loved entertaining. I guess if you start out with the idea that cooking is fun, easy, and simple, you are already halfway there. With that boy's question, I suddenly remembered the first time I had that amazing happy feeling of being in a meditative state whilst shopping for food and cooking. It all happened in Paris when I was in my twenties. I worked for a Danish clothing company, and

I spent a lot of my time on the road, sleeping in hotels, and eating in restaurants, and at the end of the week, I longed to come home. I dreamed about going to the market—the French really know how to display food, and the selection is amazing. I love it, real people selling real food that they take pride in. I would always get carried away and come home with so much food, it was impossible for me and my husband to eat it all—so why not invite a few people over?

In our house, we have an "open door, open table" philosophy—there is always room enough and food enough for a few extra guests. I truly enjoy when we go from being just four people to being twenty—and a few dogs roaming around, maybe—for dinner. I find that these simple, casually planned meals are often the ones with the best atmosphere around the table.

previous pages **FAMILY KITCHEN** Our kitchen is the heart of our house—a constant warmth beats from here. It's where everything starts and ends every day. A large table enables our "open house, open table" policy to be easily applicable.

far left **FEEL THE LOVE** I adore coming to a friend's place where I can see that thought and love has gone into setting the table—when you feel welcome, the whole atmosphere around the table always goes up a notch. Make it special with colored plates, pretty glassware, decorated napkins, and fresh flowers on the table. They don't have to be grand or expensive to capture a festive feel.

left **WHY DO UGLY WHEN YOU CAN DO PRETTY?** Place the cleaning products that you use so many times a day in a pretty container. If you make sure there is color around your kitchen sink, it makes you feel good, whatever the time of day.

"Love and light are what you get in this dining area adjoining the kitchen. When your kitchen and dining area are closely connected, you often never get any further, so make sure you are surrounded with fun, funky, and functional items."

AT THE TABLE I would love to have dinner around this table—it is inviting, light, and open. The essence of cooking, eating, and sharing is a table for young and old—a white, shiny table and splashes of colorful chairs are just perfect.

left **TEA OR COFFEE, SIR?**
If you have space for it, it is nice to have a little breakfast section in your kitchen—or a coffee and tea station. It's practical as it keeps drink-making activity away from the main cooking zone—this station is also inviting, as everything is laid out in an attractive way.

opposite, left **IF YOU'VE GOT IT, FLAUNT IT** Keep all your beautiful kitchenware out in the open. It's great to look at, and it is so easy to access and so practical at the same time—a complete win-win situation, in my book.

opposite, right **TOTAL BE-TRAY-AL** I have a thing for trays. When I host a party, I like to set little groups of food up on different trays. It gives a nice organized visual overview, and at the same time, it is easy to move things around.

Loving your kitchen

Home is where your heart is, and my heart is in the kitchen. The kitchen seems to be the center of activity in our house. It seems funny that in earlier days, the kitchen was as far away as possible from the living quarters so no one would be disturbed by any smell or noise. Nowadays, coming home to the smell of homemade bread or a lovely roasting chicken is thrilling.

In Scandinavia, many families have a penchant for making the kitchen and dining area into one big living space—often referred to as a conversation kitchen. It's a big room where everybody can do their own thing at the same time while still being together. The children can do their homework, paint, or play games at the dining table while you are chopping away in the kitchen.

This is what we have in our house too. I love to cook while friends are lounging around—sipping a glass of wine, chatting, laughing, catching up. On many evenings, we don't get further than the kitchen/dining area. Evenings like that are very informal and relaxed, and the conversation is the same.

After a fun evening like that, I am always fully recharged and very happy. For me, the kitchen truly serves multiple purposes—it is the room where I can be creative, trying out new ideas or cooking up old favorites. It is where I can relax and recharge, as it can be pure meditation for me kneading dough for a lovely rustic Italian bread, or I can let out any aggression and frustration from the working week by vigorously chopping up lots of vegetables for a nice minestrone soup. Occasionally, I allow my inner girlie spirit free rein, making fabulous cakes and desserts in endless pink shades. Or when the mood demands it, I have fun whipping up crazy cocktails and strong drinks for myself and my friends.

CREATE A KITCHEN YOU LOVE TO BE IN

Functionality is the key word. You must be practical above all—it must be easy to work in your kitchen, or you will never enjoy spending time there. Ensure easy access to shelves, cupboards, drawers, and so on—the things you use every day must be right at hand when you need them.

✳ **Be good to yourself,** and serve your food in plates and cups that make you smile.

✳ **Create an area** where several people can hang out in your kitchen while you cook, if at all possible.

✳ **Add a few stools** so it is easy for your guests to sit and sip a glass of wine or give a hand with the chopping or stirring.

✳ **Choose a strong, resistant material** for your countertop so you don't have to worry about getting it stained, burned, or scratched.

✳ **Stay clutter-free**—only keep what you use regularly.

✳ **Twice a year, go through everything** in your kitchen, and the stuff you haven't used should be sold or given away.

✳ **Light is important** both for illuminating working areas and for creating atmosphere, so if it doesn't come into the room naturally, make sure you add plenty of light fixtures exactly where you need them.

✳ **Install glossy units** in bold colors, or paint existing wooden units in the base color of your chosen palette.

above **FUNCTIONAL INDUSTRIAL** I find that having two workstations opposite each other is ideal for working in a kitchen—one against the wall with the stove and a freestanding island in front of it. But hey, this works well for me. The important thing is to organize your kitchen around the way you function.

left **FUNK UP THE VOLUME** Open- and glass-fronted shelves and wall cabinets allow you to spot anything you need in an instant and look amazing too.

opposite **STAND STRONG** With a freestanding workstation, you create a great energy flow in your kitchen. One side can be used as a small bar area for those who are not cooking.

"The open kitchen often serves as the central room for a lot of families. Keep the basic items simple and add the humor here and there, with decorative devices."

"Play with colors that lift your spirits and make you smile. Add a colorful rug to your kitchen to provide instant warmth and some bold comfort. Cooking should always be a pleasure, not a chore."

Your kitchen says a lot about you and whether food plays an important part in your life. To me, a good kitchen is one with a heart, one where everybody is welcome, where light comes in and there are a few chairs for friends to hang out, and where they can perhaps also chop along with you. Everything must be easily accessible, with a good workstation and a cooktop and oven that work like crazy. Utensils that work and look good at the same time are the best. Apart from my rice cooker and perhaps my crème-brûlée burner, I don't think I have any ugly items in my kitchen.

Food plays a vital part in my family's life—sharing food, cooking together, cooking for the people we love. I truly believe that good people love good food—I find it difficult to hang out with someone who does not care about what they eat and drink. I can really fly high on a simple good meal or a beautiful glass of wine. Buying seasonal vegetables and fruit, the little shrimps that are the first signs of spring, the new potatoes of the season, strawberries in summer—it gives me a runner's high right there just thinking about these lovely ingredients and what I can do with them.

left **OPEN HOUSE, OPEN MINDS, OPEN HEARTS**
It is very welcoming when you have the kitchen and dining area connected—it gives a good flow to a house and a great energy. Start with painted shiny floors and colorful practical plastic mats on the floor, and let the fun begin as you add in all sorts of wonderful accessories and utensils to brighten your life.

"When it comes to creating colorful kitchens, go with your heart and choose the colors that make you sing, literally. Introduce bold patches of color on backsplashes and make sure you love your choices."

opposite MAKE A SPLASH
You need protection behind a cooktop to deflect splashes and spills. Tiles are always practical, and as this is only a small area you can afford to be bold. A selection of chairs and stools in all shapes, colors, and sizes next to the kitchen counter makes sure that the cook can be kept company or closely observed at all times and adds further zing to the color kick.

SMALL BUT INTERESTING
Use a flamboyant wallpaper on the back wall, and then order a piece of Plexiglas to size and fix it over the wallpaper. That way, you can easily keep the wall clean—and you can also change the wallpaper easily according to your mood. One wall of wallpaper will provide you with some flexibility if you feel like changing up and replacing it with a different color theme altogether.

"Making a display using the colors you love is a great way of bringing absolute joy to your kitchen and creating a warm feeling for all your visitors."

VITAL SIGNS I love coming into a kitchen where there are signs of life and laughter, where you can see that cooking is actually being done and children have their drawings on the fridge. Open and welcoming rooms make you just want to settle in. Kitchens where you cannot see if it has ever been used or lived in I find very intimidating—homes are for living.

Show it, use it

Why buy something ugly if you can buy something great and colorful? But of course, it must be functional. I always go for the pink vegetable peeler, the funky-colored can opener. And even if they spend their everyday lives in my kitchen drawer, I still enjoy using them and looking at them when they come out.

If you've got it, flaunt it. That's one of my abiding principles, at least when it comes to beautiful, colorful kitchenware. My sister and I inherited a beautiful dinner set of Royal Copenhagen porcelain when we were quite young, and we could not understand what a treasure this was at first. When I moved to Paris at age eighteen, I took it with me and it became our everyday dinner set, and I finally understood what an amazing gift it was. I am still using these old hand-painted items mixed in with melamine plates. Everyday magic for me is using everything that I have and not saving it for special occasions. Over time, RICE has invaded my kitchen and my shelves. I always make things I would love to have or use myself.

If you surround yourself with colorful items, it is a pure joy to have open shelves. Some people worry that everything becomes dirty and dusty or covered in grease when standing on open shelves. I really do not think this is an issue. When you have open shelves, you see everything you have and so you are inclined to use it all regularly. It is a good idea to do an annual cleanup of the kitchen shelves anyway, just as you would do in your wardrobe. If you have not used something for a year, you might consider giving it away or selling it. Adding in further layers of color on different surfaces, such as crocheted accessories and pillows plus cotton aprons and vivid lamp shades, will complete the layered effect.

opposite, left THE WHOLE PACKAGE Tea and coffee are often sold in such attractive packaging they don't need to be stashed away. Keep them right there in front of you on an open shelf dedicated to your favorite beverages.

opposite, right NO MORE GRAY DAYS With a kitchen shelf like this, it is just blue skies ahead. For maximum impact, keep the shelves white so the colorful pieces can create their own palette. For added texture, introduce small vases of flowers or a pile of favorite fabrics to make a vivid still life that brings beauty to the eye of the beholder. Even Cinderella would have to smile at the bright red feather duster.

right SIZE DOESN'T ALWAYS MATTER You can cook up a storm in the smallest kitchens—openess in the room makes great integration with the dining area. An old wooden table suits a world of kitsch and glamorous colors—powerful contrasts always work well.

"Single items such as lights, tables, and chairs will add individual punchy color."

PICTORIAL VEGETABLES CHART

KEEPING COLOR FRONT AND CENTER

Colorful kitchens make light work of cooking and cleaning chores. If you've chosen pretty plates, dishes, and glassware, why hide their light under a bushel—or at the back of a cupboard? Put them on display so they look good even when not being used.

✳ **Open shelves will guarantee** that you know exactly what you have and inspire you to use it all. No more forgotten and neglected treasures.

✳ **Mix utility and tableware** with a few funky objects, to add a little humor to your kitchen and put that smile on your face.

✳ **Cabinets with glass doors** are another great way to store your kitchen paraphernalia while keeping track of all your stuff.

✳ **A container for utensils** placed next to the stove ensures that ladles, spatulas, and scrapers are just within reach.

✳ **Try to always go for color and quality** in all your kitchen utensils. Even if they live in your drawers, it is great to look at them many times a day when you reach for another tool.

✳ **Choose accessories in gelato colors** for added pizzazz on your countertops. Mix and match pistachio, baby blue, and pale pinks for an outdoors palette, or go vibrant with reds, purples, and deep yellows for richer definition.

✳ **Make sure there is color** in and around your kitchen windowsill. It frames the view and makes you feel good, whatever the time of day.

✳ **Mixing together old and new** items around the room, such as Royal Copenhagen porcelain with contemporary melamine tableware, is always unexpected and exciting.

opposite **CANDYLAND DISPLAY** Create a delicious moment with handmade Italian tableware nicely nestled in the shelves. After each time you use them, you can create a new favorite mix of colors by placing the plates differently.

GLAMOROUS SHELF LIFE Easy access to your favorite tableware is essential—with a glazed-door cupboard, you get to look at all your lovely things and at the same time extend your kitchen shelves in a visually pleasurable way.

left HAPPY COOKING Put your favorite cookbooks on display, and if you lack inspiration help is nearby. When you place colorful tableware and beautiful books on shelves and small tables, they become pieces of art on your walls.

opposite, above RETRO STORAGE Collecting old tins and cans is a great sport, and often very inspiring patterns and prints come to the surface. If you want to break up the shabby-chic kind of look, it is a good idea to mix in a modern material such as some plastic or melamine to the display.

opposite, below PERSONAL PARADE Add a primary painted storage shelf as a statement piece, and display a personal collection of family mementos for good measure. Even the small things in life can—and should—bring you joy.

Be your shelf, no matter what they say

I know I keep telling you that there are things that I love, but I do, I do, I do love shelves and windowsills. I lived in Paris for fifteen years, and in French apartments and houses you never find windowsills, and the windows always open inward. This was not a lot of fun for me.

In Denmark, we all have windowsills. In the dark evenings when you go for a walk, you can see all the lovely items people have chosen to place on their windowsills *pour le plaisir des yeux*—just to please the eyes, both from inside and outside.

I am crazy about surfaces where you make little worlds and display some of your favorite items or practical open shelves where you can place storage containers or kitchen items. I am not one for hiding things in cupboards—perhaps because I am not a

natural-born organized person, alas. I know my own limitations, and I know that I am not able to control my mess if I have too many closed cupboards where I can just shove it all in and forget about it.

Aside from being functional, shelves are also very nice to look at—for me, everyday magic can be a neat stack of colored linen out in the open or when I take my cups out of the dishwasher and suddenly I see a great new combination of colors.

Creating storage that feels right for your space is often a matter of adapting old or existing furniture. It's planet-friendly and ecologically satisfying to repurpose old or battered pieces. Give them a new lease on life by repainting, adding decorative motifs, and finding ways to position individual pieces in interesting ways in a room.

J'AIME CETTE PIÈCE.

left OPEN AND HONEST
This hole in the wall used to host two refrigerators and two ovens when we moved into our new house. I chose to change the space into a nice open cupboard and had some large shelves made by a carpenter. Inside I applied a striped wallpaper with a nice ribbon look—and now I am in love. These shelves host two of my fetishes—cookbooks and vases. The wall sticker says "I LOVE THIS ROOM," and wall stickers never lie.

opposite MY KITCHEN, MY PLAYGROUND Every item on my shelves is used almost every day and at least once a week. I am missing a few cabinets in our kitchen, as we dedicated the space to having two dishwashers, and thus I needed space for all my different ingredients. I have made a pantry of baskets—in one, I have all my sweet things for baking and jam-making, in another all things for Asian cooking and sushi making. I am happy when I am here.

"Gather together all your favorite plates, pitchers, and condiments, and line them up in rows. You can see what's what, and you will be reminded why you bought every piece each time you use it."

A place at the table

Visual everyday magic is easy to create around the table. In modern times, gathering around the table has often become the only time during the day when the whole family is physically together. If you make a tiny effort—a little flower in a vase, nice napkins, place mats, or a tablecloth—it does add that little extra lift to your day.

I always notice and appreciate it when I am visiting someone and I can see that some love and thought has gone into the table setting. Even if you are just popping by for a simple pasta dish, it somehow lifts the atmosphere and the conversation when you can see that someone has made an effort for your sake. And it also adds magic to the food. Food always tastes better when attractively served.

My grandmother lived alone for many years, and she taught me the importance of looking after yourself—meaning that every day she cooked herself a good, warm meal. And even if she was dining all alone, she still used her best silver, set a beautiful table, combed her hair, and sat down to enjoy her meal.

I am very loose and relaxed about many things but merciless when it comes to table setting. Even my children have been taught from an early age how to set a proper table—to put the knives and forks in their right places, to fold the napkins and place the glasses correctly. It is nice to look at and pleasing to sit down to.

But setting a correct table does not mean you have to go all dull and beige. It is easy to funk it up by mixing the colors of your tableware. Or have some fun, lighten the mood, and add a few childish touches by inviting Mr. Dinosaur—a small plastic toy—to watch over the meal or by placing a sweet soap-bubble butterfly at each plate instead of the usual name card.

opposite, left **FOOD TASTES BETTER WHEN YOU SHARE** Use masking tape to package up each place setting and write little welcoming words to your guests. "Remember to dance"—"party like there's no tomorrow"—"I have missed you"—"I love having you here" . . . whatever jumps to mind.

opposite, right **WHITE GONE WILD** Keeping a white base on chairs and tables allows you to go a bit more crazy with pillows on the chairs and a bright pink cupboard. The frames on the back wall help close in the space to a confined cozy area in the middle of the room.

right **ALL-IN EFFORT** Considering the color of the chair pillow and table setting to fit each person is truly going all in. The black-and-white rug plays well against the colorful table, keeping it from going overboard. The white and lacy look of the pendant keeps it light instead of being too overwhelming, despite its size.

DINING IN STYLE

Create an everyday dining space that is at once simple but inviting. A dining area can be dressed in any number of colors according to time of day or what kind of entertaining you are doing, from a summer lunch to a cozy evening dinner for friends.

✳ **Introduce color** on movable objects such as tableware, lamp shades, pillows, and place mats. Then you can mix and match or change up according to your mood.

✳ **Happy diners** love flowers at the table. Make individual arrangements for each guest using his or her favorite color.

✳ **Chunky pillows** provide additional seating and a sense of comfort on wooden benches.

✳ **Make sure the vases** are as interesting as the china and glasses and they complement any colorful food you serve to guests.

✳ **In the dining area,** try to include echoes of the colors that occur in the kitchen.

✳ **Large lamp shades** anchor the dining area visually and start the color ball rolling.

opposite **COLOR COORDINATED** The deep jewel colors of the chair cushions are carried through into the place mats and china. You could keep to one color per place setting or mix them up as here.

right **COZY AND INTIMATE** A tablecloth in blue-jeans denim sets a jaunty base for the colorful crockery. The papier-mâché lamp shades add a wonderful warmth and echo the rug—how can you not feel happy around this table?

Choosing tables and chairs

Choosing a table and chairs for your dining room or kitchen is fun, and the options and possibilities are endless. Whether you go for flea-market treasures or high-end purchases is a matter of personal taste—and wallet size—but these two styles can easily be blended into a funky mix. Try the chairs to make sure they are comfortable to sit in. The only rule is to make sure that the size of the table and the number of chairs fits the room comfortably. Trying to cram a table seating for twenty-four people into a tiny kitchen is rarely a great idea.

I like to mix materials and team up a wooden table with chairs in a different material. If you mix different styles, make sure that the table and chair height match each other, so you still feel comfortable when seated. You can also go all in and pick a selection of different chairs and paint them in individual colors or perhaps give them new upholstery—in that case, you should keep the table in a simple, clean style to avoid a messy-looking result. Or keep the chair color neutral and use bright chair pillows for color splash.

right **CENTER OF ACTIVITY** This table is actually my working-at-home table. It is also the table we use for playing cards and games and making big puzzles, and it becomes an extra dining table when we hold big parties—I sometimes make it the children's table. It is a luxury to have a room like this, where you do not need to pack everything away to make room for dinner. A large mirror gives depth and contributes to the different visual effects in a room.

above left **COUNTRY CHARM** Mixing different chairs around a table creates a relaxed bohemian look—subtle yet with distinctive splashes of color.

above **KITCHEN DINING** If you set up a half wall in wood panels, you get a nice cozy look and at the same time a small shelf to place candles and decorative items on.

left **SHINY, HAPPY KITCHEN** You can almost hear the children playing and the food sizzling in this cozy kitchen. To change the look quite easily, place different colored floor mats and another tablecloth. This small effort immediately has a dashing new effect.

"Painting the occasional wooden chair or stool in a color that features elsewhere in the same or adjoining rooms allows you to carry the color story through."

LET ME ENTERTAIN YOU
This is my kitchen/dining room—and my favorite area in our house. Lots of laughter and chatting go on in here. This table screams for more people, and a long table with extra chairs makes it easy to be spontaneous and invite a few extra people to stay for dinner.

HAPPY HOME MAKE

friendly table settings

Instead of using ordinary place mats, you can use decorative masking tape to make pictures to mark each individual table setting. I made a branch with a bird—only your imagination limits the fun.

Use masking tape directly on the plates and write some words of wisdom as well as a name—this gives a lovely personal touch. Add a little bird and a few pom-poms to small branches, or cut a nice scrap of wallpaper or cardboard and use it as name tag.

opposite **FAMILY FRIENDLY** Enjoy the mix of time periods in this table setting, with three generations meeting up for a great night. Vintage china plates are mixed with ultramodern melamine and colored glass and contemporary china. Flowers picked fresh from the garden are placed in individual vases, and a child's pottery tortoise meanders along happily among them.

right **BEAUTIFUL BUFFET OF HEALTHY SNACKS** A light stomach creates a light atmosphere. You can echo the fruity colors in your serving dishes or go for glorious contrast. Use half a watermelon as a vase— just stick in the flowers and they will drink the watermelon juice.

Things I love for cooking and dining

1. Colorful baskets in natural materials made on the beautiful island of Madagascar—in my kitchen, I use them as an organized pantry. *2.* Be melamine forever. Every time I empty my dishwasher, I enjoy stacking my beakers in different ways and it always amazes me how they all fit into each other in their own mixy-matchy way. *3.* A watermelon vase is cute and quirky as a table decoration *4.* A good everyday-magic trick is to always keep a bottle of Champagne nicely chilled in your fridge—you never know when it will come in handy. Have beautiful jeweled glassware to drink it from. *5.* Miss Tea, a little white poodle, has inspired several RICE collections in the past years—there is something about a dolled-up poodle that appeals to my sense of humor.

1. I love having my cookbooks on display, and all my vases as well. When we moved into our new house, I said that my new principle was one item in, one item out. *Mon dieu*, that is a hard promise to keep! *2.* Tea and sugar corner—packaging is king. *3.* I love this remake of an old classic Danish shelf in a raspberry color. I use it for eggcups and bottle openers—perhaps not the most logical of mixes, but it looks nice and it somehow works. *4.* Make jam, and put it in nice jars with a little handmade sticker for glasses filled with love—a very personal present when you are invited somewhere. *5.* I have a thing for animals—I do find them very funny. An ostrich is a big, proud bird so used as a knob on a drawer it just works—fun, humor, and function.

Opposite, clockwise from top left: Use an étagère for cookbooks—it looks good and it is practical. I read cookbooks like some people read novels; I rarely use a complete recipe but simply let myself be inspired; I love the mix of several generations both around the table and in the table settings—my grandmother's wedding plates, mini plastic side dishes from Thailand, handmade Italian ceramics. I like to imagine that things can talk together—close your eyes and think of the stories that could be told; Doing the dishes is a lot less boring when you have colorful things to wash up and look at. If it is possible to do the dishes with a view, go for that option; A typical Indian metal shelf works well in a small kitchen—it is narrow and yet holds quite a lot of things.

Sleeping, bathing, dreaming . . .

. . . in beautiful bedrooms and bathrooms

When you think about it, bedrooms and bathrooms are in fact some of the most private and personal rooms of all, whether you are an adult or a kid. These are places where you literally strip down in every sense of the word, physically as well as mentally, take off the day, and recharge.

Just because you only spend time sleeping or showering in these rooms does not mean that these are spaces to be neglected. In fact, these should almost be the rooms with the most attention paid to them. A lot of people tend to slightly overlook these rooms when it comes to decorating, but even if they are mainly for your eyes only that does not mean they should go unnoticed. A good sleep is essential to keep your energy level at the top. And a nice bath can clean mind as well as soul. So you owe it to yourself to get the best out of these two places in order to get the best out of you.

These are also the rooms where a lot of our personal things live— creams, makeup, yesterday's attire, the odd hairpin on the bedside table, and last year's best seller under the bed, long forgotten. Oh yes, show me your bathroom cabinet and I will tell you who you are!

A more personal feel in the decor comes with the territory, and so it should. The main purpose of these rooms is that you should feel comfortable and at ease. Use storage baskets so you do not have a hundred bottles standing around attracting dust and looking messy.

When it comes to children's bedrooms, they should reflect the personality of the inhabitant, not the latest trend. Children's rooms are even more private and personal, as they keep all their treasures and knickknacks, the entire content of their lives here—plus a child undergoes amazing development all the time and his or her private space should evolve with him or her. In regards to the overall look in the room, you can easily liven it up with an "ageless" wallpaper— select a color palette and stick to it. If you set out the large lines, the child can add his or her personal touch afterward.

previous pages **HAVEN** Calmness in a bedroom is essential for a good night's sleep, but a lovely vintage-style wallpaper with birds can still funk it up without becoming too overwhelming. White is the base, and colors are added in selected doses.

opposite, left **FEEL CONNECTED** When you close your eyes for a second and mentally reconnect to your bed and your bedroom, you need to get a warm, happy feeling inside—if you don't, it is time to change a few things. Surround yourself with a few personal items that bring you joy.

opposite, center **IN THE FRAME** This pretty corner is in a large bathroom. Play around with photographs and mirrors in different frames.

opposite, right **EXHIBIT YOUR JEWELRY** Make sure you do not forget all the wonderful treasures you have. Acrylic boxes and drawers are almost made for this purpose— you can see it all, and it takes up little space.

right **ALL ABOUT YOU** If you like to read in bed, where do you put the books? A bedside table can only hold so many. A high shelf takes up little space but holds plenty of books. A lamp with a soft glow and a nice collection of photos and knickknacks in a few colors above the headboard create a personal feeling.

Dream on

I love Danish author Karen Blixen and her thoughts on dreams—she said that she was always longing to go to bed because her dreams were so exciting and interesting. For me, a bedroom works best when it is very pure and simple, not too many things or colors. This leaves room for big colorful dreams.

If you read a bit about feng shui and believe in it (as I do), it says it's a good idea to avoid too much clutter in the bedroom—no stuff hidden under the bed, on top of cupboards, and so on. If you live in limited space, this can be a challenge. My advice would be to buy some nice baskets and store things in them, so it at least looks tidy.

It is important to have lots of fresh air in the bedroom and to feel comfortable in your bed—we spend so many hours there. I like a simple bed with an attractive padded headboard so I can sit and read comfortably. Lighting is also extremely important—a pretty lamp that is easy to turn off and gives great reading light is essential. It sounds like obvious advice, but I have been to many houses where this has not been a priority. Very often the bedroom is the room in the house that gets the least attention, and this is a mistake.

Every country has its own preferences when it comes to shapes and sizes of duvets and bedding. In Denmark, we are convinced that we have found the ultimate way of sleeping, and we are known to travel the world with our quilts and even our pillows. My French husband was really surprised the first time we had visitors from Denmark who had brought their own quilts for their child. And when we had just met, we went camping in a really small tent for four months in Mauritius, and I rolled up with my backpack, one pair of shoes . . . and my quilt! He thought I was a bit crazy, but today I am sure he has converted and would go to extremes to bring his own duvet along. And when our children were born, we also took their little quilt along everywhere—I remember feeling quite envious when I saw them cuddling up in their soft comforters.

opposite, left PRETTY WALLS I love beautiful wallpaper in a bedroom—and nothing else on the wall. Keeping it simple, with just a few well-chosen items and no clutter visible to the eye, is key to calmness in the bedroom.

opposite, right TEXTILE TREASURES Mix and match a bunch of blankets and bedspreads, and add a few nice rugs on a painted floor—it does not take much to give a very personal touch to your bedroom.

right LIGHT FANTASTIC As well as thinking about the pretty things, make sure you always have good lighting next to your bed. I have slept in many guest rooms where you have to get up and out of the bed to turn off the lights—really not very relaxing. This floral-shaded green lamp does the job and looks charming too.

"While I'm a great believer in display in the kitchen and other rooms in my home, in my bedroom I seek a calmer atmosphere. You need to get clever with storage so you can keep clutter at bay."

left **WALK RIGHT INTO MY CLOSET** In our bedroom we have hidden the clothes behind a half wall and installed a lot of open shelves, which most of our clothes lie on. The antique stained-glass windows form a separation between the bedroom and the clothes area and help keep all the clothes out of sight.

opposite, top left **PICK AND CHOOSE** Another great way to keep an overview of your wardrobe is a clothes rail. White shelves, white floors, and white walls accentuate the colors while providing a calm background for even the most vivid wardrobe. If you have an attic bedroom, why not dedicate the awkward eaves space to storing your clothes?

WHAT YOU NEED IN YOUR BEDROOM

If you give a little thought to planning the practical points as well as the aesthetic choices, you can create a bedroom that you can truly relax in—the place where you come to be soothed and refreshed, with no jarring notes or annoying drawbacks.

✱ **Keep the overall decor** toned down a notch. Your bedroom is where you recharge, so try to keep it simple.

✱ **Good lighting is important,** so place a lamp next to each bed.

✱ **If you always end the day** with a chapter or two, you must be able to sit and read in your bed in a comfortable way.

✱ **The headboard will always** be a dominant feature in a bedroom because of its size, so make sure it suits your style.

✱ **Keep a softer color scheme** than you might choose elsewhere in your home. Bedrooms are about peace and harmony.

✱ **Make sure you have** plenty of different storage solutions, so no clutter will disturb your bedtime routine and relaxation.

✱ **A good bed is the foremost** important thing to have in your bedroom. After all, you do spend a lot of hours here.

✱ **For temporary inspiration,** hang your favorite dress as a small sculpture in your bedroom—it's a nice way to remember that last amazing party or to look forward to the next one coming up.

above **GOOD MORNING** Welcome to the floor—I think most of us prefer to put our feet on a nice soft rug first thing in the morning. There is nothing worse than a cold floor to wake you up. Use colorful baskets for storage under your bed—it is all about keeping it streamlined.

left **HAPPY FEET** This is five-star luxury—a whole room, an actual walk-in closet, with a special table in the middle just for your flavor-of-the-month shoes. This is a fantastic idea on so many levels. Keeping all the shoes tidy yet within sight and near all your clothes makes it easy to mix and match your look of the day on the spot.

Dressing the bed

When entering my bedroom, being greeted by a fabulous-looking bed makes me really happy inside and all ready to jump in. The bed is where we spend a lot of hours, and no matter how fabulous it looks, it is to no avail if the bed itself is no good. I make my bed every morning—I can't stand a bed with pillows, comforters, and blankets in an unruly heap. A fabulous bedspread and a huge pile of pillows add a cozy and exotic twist to the bedroom, while a single-colored spread gives a calmer feeling to the room.

I love bedspreads in all kinds of materials, and it looks really great when you combine two or more on one bed. Another option is folding the spread so it only covers half of the bed for a looser but still tidy look. Matching pillows in neat rows or a mix of all styles in a huge pile is really just a matter of personal taste. But keep them at the head end—pillows in the middle of the bed just make it look as though it hasn't been made.

left **SLIDING DOORS** Put a nice graphic or old-fashioned wallpaper on your sliding-door cupboard—it removes the industrial look by breaking up the large plain surface and gives a nice homey touch.

opposite **HAPPY NIGHTS MAKE HAPPY DAYS** Using two different bedspreads gives a nice visual effect and also ensures that you never need to suffer from cold feet.

"If the walls are relatively neutral, a bright and bold bedspread creates a natural focal point in the room."

HAPPY HOME MAKE

fabric-covered headboards

This is such an easy way to get a headboard that visually frames your bed and at the same time is much nicer to lean against when you hang out in bed with a good book and a cup of tea. If you fancy a makeover, you can just replace the fabric.

Get a carpenter or hardware store to cut out MDF board in a shape you like—measure the width of your bed by around 30 inches in height. Buy some foam by the yard and a length of fabric, and use a nail gun to wrap the fabric around the foam and board.

"Textiles add softness and warmth to the atmosphere of the room, and a nice little side effect is that they also attenuate sounds. A headboard is a great way to make your bed the center of attention in your bedroom and also a must if you like to sit and read in bed."

left WONDER WALL It looks amazing when one wall in a bedroom is decorated in a fabulous mix of paintings, mirrors, framed embroidery, photos, paper art, and posters—it's quirky and it's highly personal. What you can do is gather your own personal puzzle of frames and place it on the floor—play with it until you find a look that works for you. Snap a picture with your phone and then just copy the pattern and hang everything on a wall.

opposite THE MAGIC BLACK CABINET This collection of treasures and books is nice and calm to look at and works well because the mix of books and smaller colorful items is visible without being overly dominant and the look is still tidy.

"The bedroom is your very own and very private space. Surround yourself with things that are meaningful to you. But do make an effort—even if it's only for your own pleasure and the one person you share your dreams with."

"Involve your children when making their rooms—life is not an exhibition, most kids do have bad taste, and you have to accept that and let them develop their own ideas. Hanging a dried flower crown and bouncy toys on the papier-mâché deer is clearly the happy child's doing."

left **IMAGINATION LET LOOSE** Children's rooms should be kept in tune with the child's age at all times. And it does not have to be a huge makeover every time. Change the bedspreads and the pillows. Paint the shelves in your kid's favorite color. Get some great pictures or posters for the walls, or a new lamp. It really does not take much to keep playfulness at its peak.

opposite, left **MIRROR, MIRROR ON THE WALL** Who's the fairest of them all? Dressing up and playing with makeup and all kinds of jewelry is fun for girls at any age. Actually, I do not think I ever grew out of it completely, to be honest.

opposite, right **PERCHING PLACE** A narrow ledge is a simple, easy way to display a selection of small bright and colorful items to their utmost advantage. And the display can change as often as the child's whims, without any damage to the walls.

Children's rooms

Bedrooms for children should instill the same calm and comfortable feeling that your own bedroom does. At the same time they should reflect the personality of the inhabitant and not just the latest trend. Kids also need an environment that is to their own personal liking, not necessarily yours.

Allow them to put their own touch on things—after all, it is a room for them to use. My son has had the strangest-looking bedroom for many years—at least in my eyes. As part of him affirming his own beautiful personality, he lives in a world without color—at first it was hard for me to accept, but now it just makes me smile.

Children's rooms often have a dual function. They have to work as playrooms as well as bedrooms. Children regularly have friends over, and they spend a lot of time hanging out in their room. Keep it tidy and well-organized from the outset. Not only are you doing yourself a favor as you will most likely be the one tidying up when they are young, but you will also hopefully be setting up good habits for the future when it becomes their responsibility. If you have a basket for every type of toy, you might be lucky and tidying up can become part of the game—cars in the garage basket, Lego bricks in the big box, Batman in the superhero tank box. It's up to you to invent a brand-new game of tidy and get them enthused—or at least amenable.

Keep the bed area a happy place where you would look forward to going to sleep. Have nice linens and cozy pillows, the beloved indispensable teddy within reach, a soft light for those who might be a little afraid of the dark, books within reach for the older child, and a great light for reading. It is, of course, your choice if you place a TV in the room—in our house, this is a big NO. We feel the kids will never come out and hang out with us if they have that option. But when we travel, we all love to lie in bed together in hotels and watch a movie.

right **SLEEPOVER** I love that my daughter's room now has two beds in it. I like that we do not need to drag out the mattresses every time she has someone for a sleepover, and it is also a great spot for me to lie and have a chat with her before bedtime. It is frequently used for girlfriend chitchat and game-playing as well. Her entire room is decorated with things that hold a special meaning to her, and she frequently restyles her shelves according to current mood.

"Make sure the room grows with the child—not in size but in the decoration. It is important for children to feel comfortable in their own private space. Age-appropriate decor and accessories are easily added or changed—repeatedly if needed."

KEEPING THE KIDS HAPPY

Childhood is such a short time that you want to do everything you can to keep playfulness at its peak. Even older children retain some of their favorite toys well into their teens and beyond. Take the cue from them when it comes to decoration.

✳ **White walls** are the perfect neutral starting point, as you can layer on plenty of colors and accessories and change up without having to do a major redecoration.

✳ **For the ultimate in lounging,** create a cozy corner using huge pillows and poufs.

✳ **For the older child,** a desk with good lighting for studying is important. They need to concentrate, so working around the dining room table is no longer the best option.

✳ **Teens often have very certain** opinions about what they like and what they don't. It tends to change every so often, but the room can easily adjust to the flavor of the month by changing bedspreads, pillow covers, and storage baskets.

✳ **Be brave and allow them to** have a go with the paintbrush, even if it's just one wall. You can mop up the spills, and it will give them a huge sense of involvement.

✳ **Wall stickers come in all sorts of** pictures and designs these days, from simple flowers to elaborate graphic designs and life-size figures. They are a great way for older children to exercise a bit of creativity as they can be simply peeled away if they get bored of them.

✳ **Do a big clean-out** two to three times a year—in consultation with your child, of course—and look at what works and what doesn't in the room.

A COZY, CHATTY CORNER How wonderful to have time and space for this—sharing your dreams and thoughts with your very best friends. The bed can easily be used as a sofa during daytime—just fill it up with lots of big and soft pillows and nice blankets to wrap up in.

above left **A ROOM OF ONE'S OWN** There is no need to be all serious about it. Play with colors and homemade art—funk it up with wall stickers and colorful textiles, and enjoy being young and carefree.

above **REAL BEAUTY COMES FROM WITHIN** But why not help it along? Make a little vanity corner with a mirror, a shelf laden with perfumes, creams, and other beauty stuff in a cute collection. With a small stool at hand, hours can be quite happily spent here.

"Shelves filled with great memories of kings and queens in kingdoms far, far away! There is no need to hide away your books—stack them as towers and mix with treasured fun items in order to create a relaxed look."

LIGHTING FOCUS A good rule to keep in mind when trying to encourage your kids to do their homework is to make sure you have a dedicated space. A desk with storage possibilities, such as drawers and cabinets where all unruly papers can be stored, is easy to keep tidy and a lot more inviting to sit down to than a messy one.

Fun with pattern

Let it loose. The rule is there are no real rules. It is a bit like cooking and many other things in life—just try out some new ideas, mixing some ingredients, listening to your gut feeling, and if you are happy with the result, that is the only thing that matters. In a child's room, this guidance is really appropriate as you can mix many colors. Of course you can try to respect the so-called boyish and girlie colors—when children are young, especially, they are more focused on this—but they most likely have their own favorite colors anyway that you always should try to include.

Wallpaper on one wall or a large wall sticker are great ways to introduce pattern, and are easy to change when their appeal fades. Children grow and change so much all the time—their needs and demands from their rooms change with lightning speed, so solutions that are easily changeable make it possible to keep up with their age.

left **PILE ON THE PATCHWORK** A room with a lot of different patterns can still have a harmonious look as long as you keep things mainly within the same color range and keep the walls, floors, and ceiling in a neutral tone. Here it is purple, green, and blue that are the main colors. Splashes of pink and orange add zest without going way over the top.

opposite **PAPER POWER** A funny wallpaper from childhood can easily remain on the wall into the teenage years—it is all about the accessories. A loud and bold patchwork blanket and few contrast color spots in the shape of knickknacks, frames, and vases give the room an age update with a twist.

FEMININE FOCUS This has everything a girl can dream of in one room. The luscious-looking bed, with lots of lounging, laughing, and chatting options. A desk for homework or heart-to-heart talks. Drawers and baskets in abundance for storage and art to express her personality. Keep things focused in sections to make it more appealing to the eye.

"Bright and bold and very personal—this teenage heaven was created with soft textiles in beautiful hues against a very neutral backdrop of white. Personality is very easily expressed through a selection of fun and favorite items."

"Think outside the norm when it comes to seating for teenage dens. A breakfast bar in the bedroom will feel very grown up for the lucky occupant, while a hanging chair is retro cool."

opposite **CALLED TO THE BAR** The high table and chairs give an airy feeling to the room. This is such a great place for gaming, enjoying a snack or just talking. Funk up the chairs with colorful pillows in mixed prints and patterns on both the seat and at the back.

right **COCOON** When we are babies, being wrapped up is said to give us the feeling of being secure. Here, it is an egg-shaped cane chair hanging from the ceiling that re-creates that feeling. This is a lovely place to read a book, chat on the phone, or just ponder on your own thoughts for a while. A tree wall sticker creates a peaceful backdrop for times of reflection. And with the green baseboards, painted flowers, and bird-embroidered textiles, the outdoor theme is held nicely together.

TO HAVE AND TO HOLD A large bookcase with lots of raffia and plastic storage baskets keeps the toys in check and is a great way of keeping like with like so they can be easily found . . . and put away again at the end of the day.

Storage for kids

Baskets can be your best friend and your worst enemy. If you keep them organized, they are magical and can keep your world together. If you have a tendency to just throw anything into them, you sometimes really need to purge, empty, and re-sort.

Baskets are especially useful in children's rooms. Make each basket the designated home for certain toys, and try to make it a game to tidy and place everything in its rightful home. Use your own and your child's

above left **AQUA AND VIOLET** Shelves, shelving, drawers, boxes, and baskets—you can never have too many in a child's room. Get out your paintbrush to make them more interesting.

above **ACRYLIC DISPLAY** These cases in vivid colors are a great way to show off your favorite teeny-tiny items or create small fantasy universes. Neon-colored objects really stand out and catch the eye immediately.

imagination, and make up funny stories and fairy-tale worlds of fun where cars sleep the best among their own kind, Lego bricks prefer to rest with the other bricks, and the farm animals are herded into their stable for the night. It is so much easier for the child if he or she knows where all the different toys are and doesn't have to search for everything. Baskets in mixed materials make ideal containers—I always love diversity in materials—but my heart belongs to raffia. The very first one we produced for RICE was for my newborn son's toys, and we still have this basket in our collection.

left **MULTITASKING** This old kitchen cabinet has been stripped of its sliding glass and is now effectively keeping track of a little girl's toys, games, beads, and everything else. Screw a peg rail into the wall just below the cabinet, and hang all the princess gowns and pirate capes on them—a perfect use for an otherwise empty space.

"If you mix lots of prints and patterns, then keep things within a range of two or three colors and just add a few extra dabs here and there. That will keep the look of the entire room together. In this room, greens and blues dominate in lots of different shades."

left **TOYS FOR BOYS**

A boy's room can be
quite colorful too—it is
not a privilege only for
the girls. Basically the
rules are the same; keep
the walls and floors in a
neutral color and knock
yourself out with colors
on the rest. Limit your
color palette, and that
will keep the look of the
entire room together.
For younger children,
a lot of available floor
space is ideal. This is
where most of the fun
happens and plans of
world domination are
formed—or at least how
to get an extra ice cream
for dessert.

Things I love in bedrooms

1. Truly quirky wall decor—like this pink papier-mâché rhino trophy. It draws the eye and makes you smile. 2. Mixing textiles with different decoration techniques. Crochet, appliqué, screen print, and embroidery all mix well together. 3. Little tableaux of favorite items on otherwise empty surfaces such as a windowsill create fun and beautiful scenarios. 4. Use all available surfaces, such as the side of a cabinet—it makes a nice break to an otherwise plain surface.

1. Nice and easy storage and organizing options for kids: glasses, cups, small buckets, mini boxes—anything to keep all the little bits and pieces in check. 2. Big, bright, and bold with humor. Appliqués on textiles can put a smile on your face. 3. Together we stand, divided we fall. Shelves painted in a nice color keep books and bugs together in an orderly fashion. 4. Floor pillows and poufs are a brilliant and easy way to have extra seating at hand for relaxed occasions.

Opposite, clockwise from top left Under the bed is not necessarily home for monsters—you can easily evict them and use all this space for storage instead; For the slightly older child, a high bed is fantastic. With a blanket and a flashlight you can create your own hideaway place. The occupant of this room might be a future mountain climber, as the wall next to the bed is decked out in colorful climbing holds; Bookshelves are not only for books. Combine them with treasures and knickknacks for a lighter and more personal look; Hooks are a great way to make use of the space below the shelf, here used for a collection of scarves.

Bathing in the senses

A bathroom is used every day—several times a day—by the whole family. I have lived in many funny places over time—and for ten years, in Paris, in a very small apartment with a bathroom that sometimes had ice inside the window in the mornings. I have this dream of a beautiful bathroom that I hope will come true one day soon.

Functionality is so important in this room. The bathroom has to be easy to maintain, easy to use, and feel good to be in. I am a spa junkie—when traveling in Asia, I have been to some really great spas, and I always take mental notes of what works and what doesn't. The Asian look works wonders for me in Asia, but somehow not in Denmark. Instead, I would love to give my ideal bathroom a poetic and playful yet modern and soft colorful touch.

Installing a new bathroom with all-new appliances and fixtures is a very costly exercise, so most of us have to make do with what is already there and then play with the soft items: beautiful towels, nice soaps, and maybe one wall painted in a nice soothing color. Keep it calm with not too much clutter—just a few good bath oils and not a whole battery of half-empty shampoo bottles. Again, stand back from time to time and really *look* at your bathroom, what needs to be thrown out and what can be tidied up.

I have this amazing ability to attract and fall for all sorts of creams and strange things that regularly need to be thrown out because the bottle is half-empty and the contents have become stale. I say to myself, "OK—one in, one out" when I buy and put something new in the bathroom, but I seem to be very easily persuaded into forgetting the "one out" rule! I do like to put fresh flowers in the bathroom—it is such a nice thing to do for yourself. Often we take better care of the areas in the house where we have visitors coming by than we do the places where we only come ourselves.

far left **PINK MY RIDE** It doesn't take much to change the look of a classic bathroom—paint the frame of a mirror and the wooden base where the sink is placed and you are back in the funky business with just one bucket of paint.

left **MARVELOUS MINT** In our collections, minty blue is always a hit— "Grandma Elsie's Silk Blouse," we call it. My beloved grandmother had a silk blouse in this particular shade. This color works everywhere and is a great shade to start with if you want to move into a more colorful world.

CHROMATIC HARMONY
The whole white world and some colorful details keep it simple and clean-looking in your bathroom. In this bathroom, the colors of all the decorations and even the colors on the soap-bottle labels are represented in the towels—binding the items together.

INDULGE YOURSELF IN A BEAUTIFUL BATHROOM

Your bathroom usually has to work hard in limited space, often serving the needs of several people. A practical approach pays off to make it functional, but you don't have to forgo a display of personality.

✳ **You might yearn for a Zen-like** calm space, but this sort of clinical look usually only works if you have high-end expensive fixtures—otherwise it can be soulless or, worse, shabby.

✳ **Keep the overall look tidy** with storage options for all your bits and pieces. Signs of life and activity are good, but clutter is bad.

✳ **Towels in bold and bright colors** or printed designs add a splash of vibrancy.

✳ **Avoid having lots of empty** and half-empty jars and shampoo bottles—just keep the essentials at hand.

✳ **Work with what you have** if you cannot afford to change it, and concentrate on the things you can change to make the room truly your own.

✳ **White walls and white tiles** are the perfect base—cheap, cheerful, and clean-looking.

✳ **Avoid precious artwork** in the bathroom as steam will play havoc with it, but basic prints and family snaps in colored plastic frames are a fun idea for adding personality.

✳ **Mirrors are essential** in the bathroom for shaving, doing your makeup, or checking you've flossed your teeth properly, but they can also help to bounce light around a small space, and their frames offer decorative opportunities for adding more color.

above **IN SINK** It is practical to have two sinks in your bathroom if you have the space—it gives room for a few people at the same time.

left **UP THE ANTE** Storage options in very small bathrooms can be a challenge, but place some shelves high on the wall, so they are out of reach of water splashes from the shower, and use colorful towels to brighten up the look of the whole room.

SMALL BUT WELL ORGANIZED This bathroom is just what I like—simple, functional, and easy to be in. Even the whole family could spend time here together—one chatting on the bench, one in the shower, and one putting on a bit of makeup. Baskets under the bench house all the towels, and the laundry baskets are a brilliant way to make efficient use of the space under the sloping wall.

Splash around some color

A new bathroom is a big investment that few of us get to do very often. Making the best of what you already have works just as well. Once a year, you could decide to change the color of some of the walls in your bathroom—even changing just one wall gives a total feeling of newness to a room. Start out with one wall in a nice aqua color; it gives a very clean and spalike feeling. You will see—it is not a big deal, and it gives a great feeling of renewed energy.

I love moving house because it forces you to clean up and throw out a lot of accumulated junk—it creates a lift of mood and stirs up your way of living in your own home. A cheaper and easier alternative to moving is changing a few accessories and switching things around—this is also an amazing energy booster that should not be underestimated. Colorful towels rolled up and lying in baskets or rolled up on shelves add a nice splash of color and are functional

above **TEENY-TINY YET CUTE AND COLORFUL** A large mirror and bright details such as a pink laundry bin, soap dish, and a funky frame work wonders for a very small bathroom.

at the same time. Funky floor mats in bright colors lift even the most boring of floors. Try to keep all your creams and jars stored in storage baskets or use an étagère—it attracts less dust and looks clean and neat, but remember to sort through them once in a while and get rid of the things you do not use. Colorful baskets for laundry are easy to find room for and keep the floor from overflowing with dirty clothes. If at all possible space-wise, add a chair or stool in your bathroom—I have had some of the most interesting conversations just hanging out with my children while they are lying in the bathtub, when there are no phones or computers to interfere. I love music in a bathroom as well—singing and dancing in the shower is not overrated; it really sets a good mood for the day.

left **NARROW IT DOWN** Keep only the essentials in your bathroom—and of course twelve yellow plastic ducks go under the definition of *essential* if you have a five-year-old taking a bath every day.

"A little burner for essential oils and a few candles can spread a very nice atmosphere in the bathroom. Remember to always be good to yourself—even in the little things."

PLANT A TREE Paint the stem directly on the wall or, as in this case, the cabinet doors, and use lots of different printed papers as leaves—a great way to doll up your bathroom and have fun using your creative skills to create a unique work of art at the same time.

above **GOOD TO GO** A large étagère can hold all your diamonds—fake and real—hair clips, creams, and perfume. The advantage of using an étagère in the bathroom is that it allows more air, takes less space, and makes it a lot easier to clean as you can just lift the whole thing in one go.

opposite PAPERBACK CORNER I love this wallpaper for a bathroom—and the humorous reference to books and magazines found lying near some toilets. The piles of books frame the sink and give you plenty to read when you run through the titles while you are brushing your teeth.

right TIME TO REFLECT If you are lucky enough to have a large bathroom, you can have fun creating interesting corners. Hanging a lot of different sizes and styles of mirrors on a wall gives an illusion of the room being much bigger than it actually is and automatically creates a spot for vanity time.

Working, creating, playing . . .

. . . in inspiring spaces

Perhaps *playing* is the most essential word here—if you feel that your work is play, you become much more creative and you work increasingly efficiently. I went to this amazing retreat last summer in Italy where I did a one-week course of qigong breathwork, and my mantra for the week was stay playful.

I keep this sentence close at all times—when I wake up in the morning, I imagine it is written on the wall in my bedroom. At RICE we love to play, and the items we make are intended to be mood lifting and at the same time functional and fun. I try hard not to let my life get too serious. It is not always easy, but if you focus on play your mood tends to become lighter and more fun, and a lot of things loosen up as you go along. What you can do in your home to help this process is to add some things that make it easier to play spontaneously—a basketball hoop, some gym rings, a Hula-Hoop.

Make a skipping ring on your floor, using Japanese washi tape to mark it out. If you have a hobby, make it easy to access—keep the tools and materials you need in visible, attractive baskets so they are easy to pull out and keep progressing on. Adapt your home so it caters to your hobbies and your needs—do not follow conventions here, but follow your needs and grow with them. When your children are small you have lots of toys around, and as they grow you change your living spaces with them. Adapt your rooms to your style—not to some catalog or to what others think or expect.

previous pages **KITCHEN WITH A PLAYFUL TOUCH** Truly the epicenter of the house, this room features a kitchen, office, playroom, and dining area all in one. The bright, bold decor and the fun elements, such as the hanging rings, create a nice contrast to the industrial-looking metal cabinets, the flooring, and the heavyset dark table, making the room an explosion of playfulness.

opposite, left **PRESENTS WRAPPED WITH LOVE** The joy of giving is as thrilling as receiving. Presents wrapped with love are the best. When you can see that someone has spent time searching for nice paper, crazy ribbons, or an old photo just to make you happy, it really warms your heart. Never underestimate the power of packaging.

opposite, right **FLOUR BIN MAGIC** A genius idea is to paint and decorate tired old flour bins with fruit and flower motifs, then attach them to the wall for storing craft materials, shoes, paper for recycling, or schoolbooks. Keep them in a hallway for a creative but tidy approach to household organization.

right **SHOOTING HOOPS** Staying playful at every age is so important—adding a hoop in your house and a few balls makes sure that you take your thoughts and put them into play.

Work and create

Work, work, work . . . in today's wireless and constantly connected world, a lot of us carry our workspace with us in the form of laptops and smartphones. When you watch movies from a few decades back, the home office was a sacred closed space, which no one should disturb. But I know hardly anyone with a separate home office anymore.

When we visited all these lovely homes for this book, I asked everyone: where do you sit when you enjoy quiet time by yourself, and where do you sit when you work? The answers are mostly "Wherever I lay my laptop, that's my office," and yet everyone tends to feel connected to a few spots in their home where they are able to be more focused and mindful. There is a lot of freedom in being able to move your workplace around as you please, but sometimes it can be good to stay grounded in one spot to concentrate and fully focus. I have several places in my house where I like to sit and work. I move around a bit like a cat seeking rays of sunshine, but when I really have to write something, I sit in one specific spot at a large worktable. I need a bit of order around me when writing, but at the

same time, I draw great inspiration from down-to-earth and very off-line things—a flower in the window, my dog snoozing at my feet, the sound of my family in the other rooms, lighting a candle, and enjoying a cup of tea. This somehow helps my creative mind.

If you love being in the middle of the action—love knowing what everybody in the family is doing while you work—it is great to place your work desk in the epicenter of your home. Remember, there are no rights or wrongs but only tailor-made solutions that fit each individual. If you need to avoid temptations, you should find a room removed from noise and place yourself away from windows, facing only your own mood board. Make sure to surround yourself with things that inspire you so work is always a pleasure, not a chore.

far left **WORK IT BABY, WORK IT** A desk and a memory board in the same subtle gray color make an instant office that does not overwhelm the room.

left **INDIVIDUAL CHOICES** A creative or workspace must reflect who you are. If your creative juices flow when you look out the window, this is where you must sit.

opposite **CENTER OF ATTENTION** A small sanded-down table with a few essentials and a painted wooden stool sets the frame for this tiny corner office.

YES, MR. POSTMAN
Please bring a letter for me—a nice handwritten old-fashioned one, written exactly at this desk. I am sure only quirky words come out from the person working at this desk. At the end of the day, you can just close the desk and your office will disappear.

opposite **COOL AND CREATIVE** Keeping all your yarn and fabric scraps organized is essential so you do not waste time searching for things once you have that brilliant idea in your head of something you want to make. Pretty plastic cloth covers the desktop and is easily changed when it startis to look a little too tatty.

CREATIVE CORNERS

Creativity often comes spontaneously, so easy and instant access to a suitable space is of the essence. You don't need a big room—unless your hobby is to create life-size elephant statues! A small nook for a desk or an end of the dining room table will often do. It is all about finding somewhere you feel comfortable.

✳ **A small table or desk** where you can do your thing is great, but if you lack the room a small folding table will do and can easily be hidden behind a door when not in use.

✳ **If your workspace** is in your living room, either make it part of the space and as attractive as possible or try to find a way to partition it off.

✳ **A notice board** on the wall is great for keeping inspiration within sight. You can regularly change the display so it doesn't become stale. If you keep the same postcards and snaps up there month after month, you will stop really seeing them.

✳ **A set of drawers on wheels** can be used as extra worktop space when pulled out from under a desk.

✳ **Flip-down cupboard doors** act as a natural writing space or somewhere to pop your laptop, and can be closed up to restore the cupboard to its usual, everday shape.

✳ **A chair is important.** To avoid the distraction of a numb bottom, make sure you have suitable padding or a plump pillow.

✳ **Surround yourself with stimulation.** A few framed pictures define the space. If you want to keep things fresh, simply use washi tape to fix your current favorites to the wall.

left **GOOD DAY AT THE OFFICE** My friend Michelle is a volcano of creativity—her mind is always working overtime, and she is extremely efficient and runs several companies. Guess where her office is? A high daybed in her kitchen where she settles with her smartphone and her laptop. How wonderful is that? Office supplies are stored in pull-out drawers under the bed.

opposite **TRAYS WITH TEA AND THOUGHTS** A mini desk on a tray is perfect if your office is a daybed. I am so fond of trays, as you may have noticed. I love that you can make things look nice and at the same time be efficient, because you have all you need right in front of you.

"Your working area need not be a desk and chair. If you feel more creative sitting cross-legged on a daybed, then make that happen. You will be more productive."

HAPPY HOME MAKE

boards to take notice of

I am always amazed how people are drawn to notice boards or to magnet-mania fridges, just checking what is going on. Souvenirs, invitations, to-do notes, goals, love letters—you can frame a small world using pins or magnets.

Cover a plain corkboard with your favorite fabric, using a staple gun to secure it at the back. Or find a fancy frame you like—perhaps one you've found at a flea market—paint it a funky color, and line it with corkboard. Hang it up and you're good to go.

left **TO HAVE AND TO HOLD** A large bookcase in the middle of a room can hold the whole family's mix of interests: creative corner, toys, books, beads, and games. The chances of staying in touch with your things and using them regularly are higher when you see them every day.

opposite, left **USE IT, SHOW IT** This metal storage board becomes a live exhibition—and a great way to keep everything nearby and categorized. Forget all about that one messy drawer where everything is jumbled up and you spend five minutes searching for a pen.

opposite, right **HIDE AND SEEK!** I love these fabulous shelves. They allow you to both show off pretty things, such as ornaments and flowers, and halfway hide away others, like storage baskets. Their graphic shape also creates an interesting look to the room.

Storage and display

To me, these two elements seriously overlap. If you have beautiful things, why hide them away? Just as in the kitchen I like to keep all my dishes, pots, and pans on open display, I like to make a feature of displays in the rest of the house. As a family, we have lots of hobbies and interests that make us who we are, so why try to hide away all evidence of human life?

Creativity and crafty corners can come in many shapes and forms, but rarely do they take up an entire room. Most creative people I know—those armed with the smart hands, the sewing machines, and the knitting needles—often keep their crafty stuff in baskets and boxes that they pull out whenever inspiration strikes. A corner in the living room or one end of a table is all that is needed. What's important is that you have the things that inspire you easily at hand. Well-organized boxes make it a lot easier to see what you have and decide what to use, and they are easy to stack away when the space is needed for other purposes. And it's important to show the evidence of your creativity too, whether it's the children's paintings,

some beautiful needlework (if that is where your talent lies), a gorgeous crocheted blanket, or just in the arrangement and styling of some of your favorite books, artwork, and ornaments.

I dream of drawing and painting, but somehow the images and lovely things that are very clear in my mind always turns out quite differently on the trip from my head down to my hand. An elephant can turn into a dog, and a beautiful flower might look like seaweed. A way for me to express my creativity is by making a nice card or beautifully wrapping a gift for a special friend—this calls for my crafty genes. I love wrapping presents in new and different ways; two presents never look the same. The joy of giving is immense.

Pretty things

I find one of the best ways to stimulate my creativity is to surround myself with lots of lovely things. Artwork, books, collections— all can add a little jolt of stimulation every day and raise a smile when you pass by. Of course, you have to be a bit choosy—if everything around you is cluttered, you will miss the subtle relationships and interplay between different pieces. And some stuff will always need to be stashed out of sight. That's where clever storage comes in.

above left **FLY, BIRD, FLY** If you like to collect things, it works well to gather them all in a small tableau, using vertical as well as horizontal surfaces.

above **MINT IS THE MASTER** A contrast-colored table is great for exhibiting your inherited pieces that are perhaps a little bit darker in tone.

Many of the most successful storage pieces are the result of a lucky find in a flea market, a beloved old glass-fronted family heirloom cupboard that you cannot bear to part with, or else sets of unloved items in a junkyard that are crying out to be rescued and revamped. Keep your eyes peeled whenever you are out and about, and spare a thought for the ugly and unkempt. Often a battered old quirky cupboard, shelving, or bins only really need a creative eye and a clever use of color or fabric to completely transform them. The satisfaction you get from creating something new from the old and repurposing period pieces will definitely bring you happiness every time you use it.

left **UNLEASH YOUR INNER PICASSO** Let your children play with paint and canvas—they are much more spontaneous and easygoing than most adults. Have a small art opening ceremony a few times a year, and change for new masterpieces. A wall like this will definitely draw a lot of attention.

right **MULTIPURPOSE LIBRARY** Come have a look in the book cupboard. This used to be an old wardrobe, but the wooden door was replaced with a glass pane and the hangers replaced with a few built-in shelves. This is a great way to stack and store your books so they are protected, but you can still find a particular title at a glance.

A HAPPY HOME IS AN ORGANIZED HOME

Get yourself set up with some well-thought-out and fun storage, and your life will run more smoothly. It will also give you the flexibility to be more creative in the rest of the space. Attractive shelves and cupboards do their job of holding all of life's necessities and look good too. What more could you ask?

✳ **Keep it well organized** so it is easy to find what you are looking for. Nothing can kill a creative moment faster than having to search high and low for that particular piece of paper or the beautiful vintage buttons you *know* you have somewhere.

✳ **Forget dull storage solutions,** and upcycle some flea-market finds to create stylish new storage pieces.

✳ **Add decoration, a new coat of paint,** unusual containers, and a good dash of imagination, and you will quickly transform any room into a happy space.

✳ **Sort your tools and materials** into different types. Set up some boxes with clear labels for all the small fiddly stuff.

✳ **Lidded baskets for larger** stuff can be stacked for minimum use of floor space.

✳ **Wall-hung storage solutions** keep clutter off the table and leave more room for all the fun but still allow you to see exactly what you got and where those scissors are.

above left **TONE ON TONE** Paint only two-thirds of a wall, and add a small wooden trim to finish the look. If you need a large cupboard to store things, you can camouflage it a bit by using the same color as on the walls. That way, it will not seem too dominant.

above **ART MAKES YOU SMART** A nice match between bowl and artwork is simple yet striking. Sometimes simple is the best way to go, especially if you have a busy piece of art.

left **WALLPAPER WONDER** Use a scrap of wallpaper to line a basic shelf; the results are just lovely, and this is an easy way to give it a personal look. When you look for old shelves in flea markets, think paint and wallpaper.

YES, WE ARE OPEN A window between two rooms gives light and perspective. This is a brilliant idea for how to create a small personal space in a room without blocking the light. Hang lanterns from the ceiling for a nice, soft light effect and gain free space on the well-organized shelf below—the ultimate win-win solution.

"Lay your cards out right from the start. In this hallway, the oversize toy soldier and bikes propped ready to go let you know straight away that fun is a serious business in this home."

left **COME IN AND PLAY WITH US** This is the first thought that comes to mind when you enter this lovely apartment. A huge wooden soldier guards the door and welcomes you at the same time when you enter the hallway.

opposite, left **DON'T GROW UP TOO FAST** That is my dream and hope for every child—that they stay carefree, playful, and fun-loving forever. Give them the tools and the toys, and you will help them on their way.

opposite, right **DESIGN-STUDIO DESK** It's a girl who lives here, one very much in touch with her inner creative goddess—just imagine the Christmas presents that can be produced at this little table.

Playrooms

Playfulness must be everywhere—that is my dream for everyone. But we can all agree that the headquarters of playfulness is in children's rooms. Every age has different needs, but if you use these now familiar three words—*fun*, *function*, and *color*—as your mantra, you can adapt this to every age and the changing needs of growing children.

My own children would only spend a small amount of time in their own bedrooms when they were young—they would play with their toys in the living room or wherever the rest of the family was. But even if the well-appointed nurseries are mostly a mother's dream come true, there are still a few good basics to remember.

Toys must be easily accessible to a small child, and there must be plenty of room to play. Storage is essential, with lots of small baskets and boxes for organizing and tidying up. If everything has a dedicated spot, mess will never be an issue. Be creative—go crazy. Make little worlds of display for all the most treasured pieces. Build a castle out of cardboard boxes. Paint a wall hot pink.

For an older child, room for playmates is a must. A quiet place to do homework without too many distractions within view is also good. A nice bed will ensure good sleep and sweet dreams. Mattresses for acrobatic fun that can also be used as beds when small guests are spending the night or as a base for great pillow fights.

For teenagers, a vanity corner is of the utmost importance (if you ask them) with a good spot for looking at themselves in the mirror for what seems like inordinate amounts of time. Make room for the fast-growing wardrobe as clothes gradually edge out the toys, and create a cozy corner where they can hang out, sharing secrets or discussing the latest football results.

HOW TO GET—AND STAY—PLAYFUL

Playing is not just for kids—it keeps us all young at heart and soul. And most of these tips can be applied to the adult playroom or creative corner in your home as well.

✻ **Using playful elements as part** of the decor encourages play for both young and old. Put climbing holds on a wall, and I guarantee that anyone who sees it will give it a go.

✻ **Include as much free floor space** as possible. It naturally invites hours of active playing. If your floors can sustain it, keep a little tricycle in the playroom.

✻ **Keep everything within easy access** of the child, so anything can be used whenever inspiration hits or the mood changes.

✻ **Keep all the little bits and pieces** well organized and stored. It is so much more fun to play and be creative if you can find what you are looking for in a heartbeat.

✻ **Masking tape for marking out** games directly on the floor is a cheap, fast, and easily changeable way to create fun and play at all times.

✻ **Hang costumes in the open,** so you can see them. Dressing up is fun and with a clear view of every gown, wand, tiara, sword, eye patch, or parrot (for the shoulder, of course), it is even better.

✻ **Display the young artist's** works for further encouragement. You never know if you are harboring the next Michelangelo.

✻ **Most important of all** is do not grow up too fast. Stay playful forever!

above **PLASTIC FANTASTIC** Hang little pieces of homemade wall art from the hands of your children on the wall in a cute lineup.

left **SKIP AND JUMP FOR JOY** It's happy hour in this wonderful room—you can create all sorts of fun games on the floor using washi tape, and they are easily changed or removed. Great for a rainy day.

opposite **SEND IN THE CLOWN** This spectacular detail is an invitation to behave like a silly, happy child. With a piece like that, there is no need to add any more. A shelf just below the ceiling is a great space for storage.

"Want to join the circus? Rooms with lots of options for the playful mind right at hand are inviting to all . . . kids as well as adults. Enjoy a skip and a jump together before climbing the wall."

Keeping it fun

All kids are different, but most of them have a natural curiosity for all things new and exciting. If you give them the opportunity, they will most likely try out anything presented to them. They can easily be encouraged to be active even when indoors—it is all about thinking up new ideas. A climbing wall is great fun, and it develops the motor skills as well. Easy access to play motivates us to make use of it more often.

Keep the fun coming—the obvious headquarters for playfulness is a child's room. Try as much as you can to place some elements of play in the room. A punch ball. A set of skipping stickers on the floor. A Hula-Hoop. A big gym ball to roll on. Hang a small swing in the room if you have enough space for it. Just use your imagination. Children of today grow up so fast, I think it is important to inspire them to play and enjoy being children for as long as possible. And remember, adults are also allowed to play and act like children. Kids love it when adults get involved and become young and carefree again.

right **THE PRINCESS ON THE MOUNTAIN** Girl power meets creative princess. It is indeed possible to combine versatile interests. Climb that mountain or indulge in dressing-up games—the trick is to think out of the box and tailor the room to the intended inhabitant.

"Utilize all the space you can. Keep floor space clear so that the children have somewhere to tip out a whole box of building bricks to find the exact piece they want. And go vertical too—so you can have them literally climbing the walls."

bonjour

Creative and playful things I love

1 2 3 4 5

1. A rotating hook with jewelry and small evening bags—which one to take today? **2.** Personal space—I love having a corner that is mine and mine only. **3.** Raffia storage with hand-embroidered details—charming and useful. **4.** No surprise—I have a serious crush on washi tape. I could washi tape my whole street and my neighbor's car if he would only let me. **5.** Walk all over me . . . no, thanks. But please read carefully and grab the words of wisdom through your feet as they get wiped on the wisecrack words. And *yes*—let's play.

1 2 3 4 5

1. This art deco bottle opener is the essence of fun, function, and beauty—it was inherited from my great-grandfather whom I never met, but I imagine his big hand opening nice cold beers for himself and his friends every time I use it. **2.** Fridge magnets—I have a thing for them. I am trying to control it but not managing very well. **3.** Books, ceramic jugs, and bowls, pictures popped on top of a cupboard—so many things to choose from. **4.** Designated storage baskets make it easy for young and old to stay organized . **5.** Flea-market finds are transformed with a bucket of paint and a scrap of wallpaper.

Opposite, clockwise from top left It's a wrap! Tie a little figurine on the ribbon, and use an old photo as a gift card on a present wrapped with love and care. It is really just small things that make the big difference between ordinary and special, and we all love to get a gift that clearly shows love and attention from the giver; Glorious and glamorous—the rule is there are no rules. Just jump into it and mix colors until you find the ones that really make you smile in your heart; Great birds and fast cars hold it all together in this little still life; Bonjour, bonjour! I like to place books and photo albums around the house in unexpected places, keeping curiosity on its toes.

Entertaining, unwinding, dining . . .

. . . and living well outdoors

In Scandinavia, you learn to appreciate the short summertime when outdoor living is possible. Living well inside and outside is a must for me. Whether your outdoor space is a tiny balcony or a big garden, I do believe that if you stay true to color, fun, and function, you can't go wrong.

I find that growing flowers in pots and baskets of all sorts of shapes and colors is the easiest way to add color in my garden, and they can easily be changed if I decide on a new favorite flower or color. I am not a very skilled gardener—I have no self-confidence when it comes to tending plants. I am a notorious serial killer of many beautiful roses and other lovely flowering shrubs and bushes—the list of killings is unfortunately long. If you were to call me to ask me to look after your garden or your plants while you are on vacation, it could really freak me out. I would much rather you called me in a panic and asked me to come round and cook for twenty people in thirty minutes—that I could handle!

However, this lack of natural aptitude does not stop me from loving being outside or loving flowers, for that matter—each summer we broadcast a lot of seeds, and I am very good at harvesting flowers in every color imaginable and placing them in well-chosen and just as colorful vases all around my house. I choose to have lots of flowerpots in every size, shape, color, and material imaginable—it makes for a great mix when you have plastic pots, lanterns, ceramic pots, and so on in one mixed crowd. When I plant in pots, it somehow feels OK that the flowers only make it through one season. When winter comes, we plant little Christmas trees or winter roses—it is necessary to have something nice to look at throughout the cold, dark season as well. Fresh herbs planted close to the kitchen and the barbecue are also a must, and what a joy it is to be able to cut a handful of fresh basil or parsley or whatever herb you prefer and throw it on the steaks or add it to the sauce.

previous pages
PERFECT SUMMER DAY
I am not sure what it is, but hanging laundry on the line outside is probably the only household chore I truly enjoy. Colors can easily be incorporated in even the most practical everyday doings. Paint the poles, find a nice colored line, and use a bright bucket for those funny-shaped pegs.

opposite, left **HOT ORANGE** A bright bench makes a wonderful contrast against a dark wall. This being my poolhouse, a row of colorful hooks for towels and wet bathing suits to dry was added.

opposite, center **FLOWERS TO GO** Lots of colorful pots with flowers create great little green corners on the terrace, and the flowers can easily be changed or moved around.

opposite, right **TRAVEL PILLOWS** Chair pads in bright colors give a true summer feeling—even to a car seat.

right **PICK UP AND GO** Cozy corners in the garden with furniture to lounge in and a parasol to provide shade are the essence of outdoor living. Mix assorted styles of furniture with pillows and blankets to create a laid-back, relaxed ambience. And have lanterns ready for when the night falls.

left **SUMMER IS HERE**
In Denmark, we have a tendency to go wild when the sun and summer arrive, spending as much time as possible outdoors. Perhaps it's because the really great summer days are few and we all know that a long, dark winter season lies ahead of us, so we are determined to stock up on vitamin D and warmth. Outdoor dinners are easily executed with lots of colorful melamine and acrylic tableware at hand. Keep a supply of summer-related toys ready for the kids, and let them roam free while the barbecue is getting ready. The whole point is to keep it easy and stress-free for all.

opposite, left **PRETTY AND PRACTICAL** Just because you have to play it safe with unbreakable dishes doesn't mean you have to play it safe with your colors. Gorgeous melamine dishes and cups in a rainbow variety of prints and colors are the perfect solution for happy outdoor eating and drinking.

opposite, right **OUTDOOR LOUNGE** An old wicker basket used as a table and a couch with soft blankets, teamed up with a bucket of flowers, creates a beautiful spot in the sun. Mix all sorts of materials and styles to give it your own personal touch.

Let me entertain you . . .

In my life, a garden is mostly about fun and friends. I don't care much if the lawn is perfect; my priority is good times spent. Being outdoors makes entertaining a lot easier and more relaxing. Friends, family, kids, dogs, and cats can run free—everybody enjoying the weather and each other's company. Be practical and prepare well before your guests arrive, and everything tends to run smoothly after that.

Something amazing happens to people in summertime—everyone seems to relax more, becomes more spontaneous, and invites each other over more often to improvised barbecues in the garden. My advice is keep it simple. Make sure you have a good barbecue and some chairs and tables that are easy to move around and can cope with changing weather. Use some plastic or melamine glasses and plates that will not break easily. If you organize your garden party like you would organize a picnic it makes the evening much more fun for you, because you do not need to race into the kitchen all the time while everyone else is enjoying themselves outside. Have a few good cooler boxes filled with lots of ice, and keep everything nicely chilled. As the evening progresses, candles and lanterns cast a lovely cozy atmosphere—add some music and the scene is set to have a bit of dancing in the moonlight. If at all possible, create a small bonfire pit: this is an excellent idea both for cooking or just lying around telling stories, keeping warm, listening to the crackling sounds of the burning logs, and, of course, for stargazing.

A tradition at my house is open-air movies on the terrace. All you need is a white wall, a projector, and two loudspeakers. Add as many good friends as you like, a few bowls of popcorn, and some snacks, plus a stack of warm blankets to keep everyone from getting cold, and you are all set up for a cuddly and cozy magical night.

KEEPING FRIENDS AND FAMILY HAPPY OUTDOORS

Having lots of little corners with a few tables and chairs makes it easy to move around in the garden, seeking sun or shade, whichever you prefer, and allows a summer lunch to progress naturally into a relaxed evening.

✳ **I love outdoor couches**—cozy corners with lots of pillows often prolong the summer evenings well into the night. If you are comfortable, why should you move indoors?

✳ **Make sure you have** lots of blankets ready for when the sun disappears. It is hard to enjoy even the best of parties if you are freezing!

✳ **Tableware that won't** break is great for garden gatherings, so you don't have to worry about drops and spills.

✳ **Chair pillows can bring new** life to your garden furniture in an instant.

✳ **Create a bonfire pit** if you have a suitable spot. You'll be amazed by the good conversation that flows around the flames.

✳ **Keep the kids entertained** well into the evening—and adults too—with games and dancing if you're feeling energetic.

✳ **In a large garden,** make the most of mature trees. I have a gorgeous apple tree that provides enough shade for a lot of people, but if you are not so fortunate, you will need to have parasols at hand.

✳ **Biting insects can ruin** the most convivial of evenings, so install a few wasp traps filled with sugar solution, and burn citronella candles to keep the mosquitoes at bay.

above **CAMPFIRE MAGIC** Bonfires are just wonderful. When nightfall arrives, it is the ultimate place for cozy togetherness and perhaps a few ghost stories while the marshmallows are toasting. Add a few lanterns to show the way back inside.

left **SET THE TABLE** A lovely combination of melamine, acrylic, and flatware is bound to make you smile inside.

opposite **IN THE PINK** When you have a table as colorful as this, a way to keep a harmonious look is to choose the same color for all the chairs and tables. That will keep it all together.

On the move

If you get the urge to get away from home, camping is fabulous and something my family and I enjoy. Many years ago, when my husband and I got married, I really wanted this fabulous old Citroen van, so I asked him *please*, do not buy me a ring, but buy me this van instead—and he did. The van has a great story to it. It used to belong to our friends Roger and Juliette from Burgundy in France. For many years, Roger used the van in his vineyards as a working

above **HAPPY CAMPERS** Being in a bad mood inside this van is difficult—surround yourself with color and fun items, and just get on the road ready for adventure. There is something thrilling about packing up your favorite things, creating your home for the summer, and then setting off to explore lots of new places.

truck, but then he decided to transform it into a mobile home. Being a winemaker himself, he decided that for a long summer holiday they required room to store 120 bottles of wine, so we are able to travel around with a complete wine cellar. On my very first trip to France, when I had just met my husband, we went camping, and this is where I first met Roger and Juliette and fell in love with them and the van at the same time. After some years Roger unfortunately had knee problems—and the van is an old lady that is not the easiest to drive if you have knee problems—so they decided to sell it. We went to Burgundy to pick it up, and they both had tears in their eyes when we drove off into the sunset after having enjoyed one of Juliette's amazing lunches.

left **STAY COOL** Spend a bit of money on a very good cooler box—it really is worth it if you intend on becoming outdoorsy for the summer and want a ready supply of cold drinks.

"This is the true story of my most favorite possession—my wedding ring on wheels. The feeling of being free as a bird and yet having all your own things around you is utterly thrilling."

HIT THE ROAD Camping and being on the road gives you that young and carefree feeling that is so vital. Only bring what you will use and need.

top **A LAYERED LUNCHBOX** Oh, the excitement— what is in the next layer? These stackable boxes are great for carrying a lot of little dishes in one go.

above **WELCOME ON BOARD** It was love at first sight—and till death do us part.

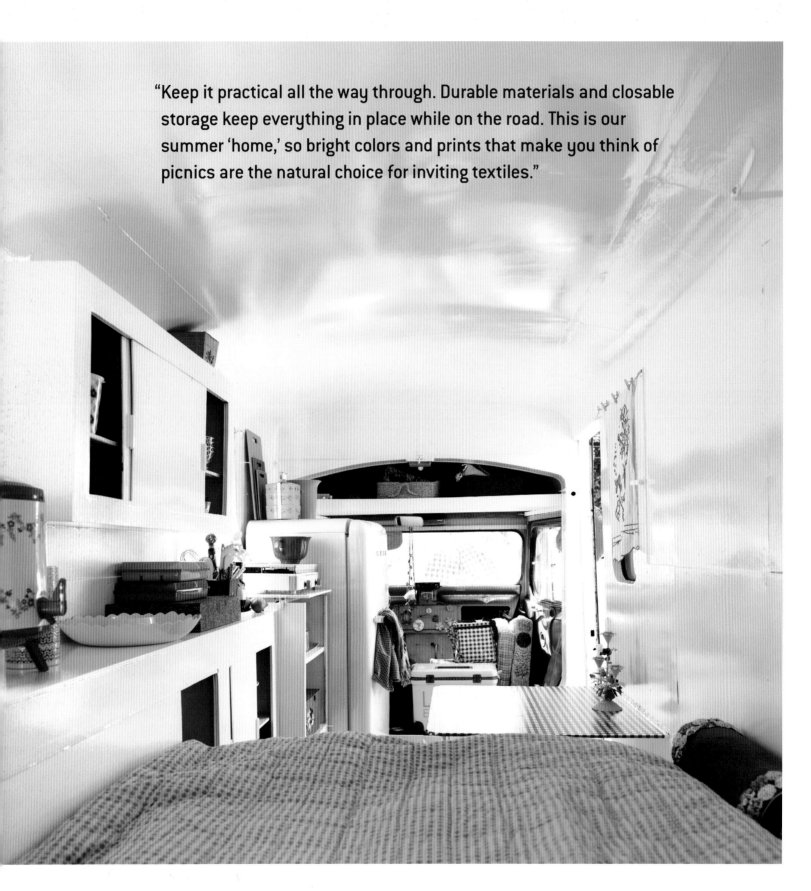

"Keep it practical all the way through. Durable materials and closable storage keep everything in place while on the road. This is our summer 'home,' so bright colors and prints that make you think of picnics are the natural choice for inviting textiles."

opposite **FREE AT LAST**
I have read and slept for hours on this bed while my husband has driven us through the French countryside—some of our best holidays have been us driving around in France. Simple living is what camping is all about—we only bring the essentials to enjoy life. The van has been painted and redecorated inside several times, always filled with every functional, colorful item that one could possibly need and ready to drive off on new adventures as soon as the weather allows it.

above **JOY RIDE** Why not decorate your car inside—the beauty is in the small details. Add some bright beads, a few pillows, and a colorful blanket. Decorate your car for Christmas or Easter—it doesn't take much and makes driving a fun experience.

above right **GET A HANDLE ON IT** Rainbow beads tied on a picnic basket are a nice eye-cleansing detail.

right **FRUITFUL ZING**
Take time to enjoy what surrounds you—such as a few lemons and limes on a red checked tablecloth. Everyday magic is everywhere you look for it. A few figs on a mint-colored plate, strawberries in a bright yellow bowl—I often choose my plate according to my food so it makes me appreciate the small, precious things in life.

Terraces and balconies

Not everyone is blessed with a garden, but terraces and balconies will also provide you with the outdoor-living feel—without the time-consuming lawn mowing. A terrace gives you the opportunity to landscape with flowerpots in all colors, shapes, and sizes. Raised beds will provide you with your own produce, and it is amazing how many things you can actually grow in just a little bit of soil. The greatest thing about this kind of garden is that you can easily change it and explore new ways of setting things up any time you feel like it.

Even the smallest balcony has the potential to become a lush garden. Grow flowers and strawberries in pots hanging from the railing. Ceramic pots for herbs will keep them in place during windy days, and a colorful plastic bucket filled with rhubarb or a few potato plants is easily moved around, assuring maximum use of a limited space. With stackable chairs and a folding table, you have built a small haven where you can enjoy the sun, drink your morning coffee while you read the paper, have a barbecue, and feel the wind in your hair.

Taller plants such as bamboo can act as shade against sun and as wind breakers, or can be placed to create some privacy if your terrace is very visible to others.

below **FUNKY FURNITURE** Furniture from flea markets can be made over to perfection with a little paint and a few pillows to accentuate the style. A row of buckets planted with flowers set on the low wall provides a little privacy from the eyes of passersby. A place to lie and daydream is quickly made with a daybed and lots of bright pillows and blankets for comfort.

opposite **DINING IN STYLE** A small foldable table can easily be moved around or out of the way if needed. A plastic rug in a cool color is great if you have stone floors that tend to get quite hot in the sun.

"A nice outdoor place for leisurely spent afternoons is a great reenergizer. Lots of pillows and throws keep you comfortable, and if any place was ever suited for resembling a rainbow, this is the one."

LIZARD LOUNGING Many a drink has been had on this terrace—garden life is about sharing, living, relaxing, and just hanging out. Comfortable couche make you want to sleep outside under the stars. I do it whenever possible for true everyday—or every night—magic.

left **FLOWER POWER** Even the smallest balcony can become a haven. A brilliant solution for all your outdoor gear is a box like this—it works as a bench during the day and stores the blankets and pillows during the night and rainy days. An old wooden crate serves as the garden with potted flowers, statues, vases, and candles. A plastic rug with a green pattern covers the concrete and creates the undergrowth. It's like having a miniature park.

opposite **BEAUTIFUL BALCONY** The wooden deck gives a terrace feeling to this tiny balcony. Opaque panes let you enjoy total privacy when relaxing in the sun. Window boxes on the outside of the railing reveal a pretty rim of flowers, and movable rail-hanging holders on the inside can be shifted around as you please. The trick is not to overflow a small space like this with too many items. Select a few nice things and enjoy the peace and quiet.

Things I love in the great outdoors

1. Tins for storing utensils. It is so much easier to find what you are looking for when it is out in the open. 2. Textiles in mixed materials and colors. 3. Canisters for food storage. No mess from all the half-empty bags of flour, rice, sugar, and whatnot when you are on the move. 4. The combination of several materials in a table setting—the practical mixed with the luxurious feeling of a fabric napkin. 5. Flowers—and lots of them! They add instant ambience to any room or table.

1. Stackable plastic chairs. Colorful, of course, and so practical to whip out without taking up a lot of space when not needed. 2. Lanterns in all shapes and sizes are perhaps the easiest way to create a cozy feeling—outdoors as well as indoors. 3. Large baskets for garden plants make it easy to create full-blooming nooks and corners in the garden in an instant. 4. A jam party with all my friends chopping and chatting! And this year, I want to host one in my garden at the end of summer when all the fruit is ripe and ready. We can all sit and chop and have a good laugh, make lots of different jams, and be creative on the labeling. 5. Acrylic "crystal" in funky colors—mix and match is a given.

Opposite, clockwise from top left A tray to carry all you need into the garden is a must and saves you a lot of extra trips into the house; Pool or no pool, your terrace gets a clean look if you gather your plants and pots in small groups; Colors for kids, colors for tables, colors for all; Soft textiles for comfort seating in contrast colors add a nice, personal touch.

RICE STOCKISTS

For all things RICE visit
www.rice.dk

To follow Charlotte's blog
visit everydaymagic.dk

AUSTRALIA
Alfresco Emporium
1021 Pittwater Road
2097 NSW Collaroy
0061 299729999
www.alfrescoemporium.
com.au

Corner Store WA Pty Ltd
147 South Terrace
WA 6160 Fremantle
0061 893363005
www.cornerstore.net.au

Lark
4a Duke Street
VIC 3460 Daylesford
www.larkmade.com.au

Mozi Mini
769 Glenferrie Road
Hawthorn 3122
Victoria
0061 3 9885 9789

BELGIUM
Huiszwaluw
Sint Elisabethplein 11
9000 Gent
0032 92332737
www.huiszwaluw.be

De Kleine Zebra
www.kleinezebra.be

BRAZIL
Aficionado
Al. Ministro Rocha Azeve.
834
01410-002 Sao Paulo
0055 1130831962

CANADA
Posie Row
210 Duckworth Street
St. John's
Newfoundland
A1C 1G5
0060 7097222544

Room 6
4389 Gallant Avenue
North Vancouver
British Columbia
V7G 1L1
0060 46288484
www.room6.com

DENMARK
Continental
St. sct. Peder Stræde 5
8800 Viborg
0045 86 61 43 24

Decorate
Middelgade 2, st
8900 Randers
0045 4190 8905

lillum Dekorations afd.
Østergade 52
1001 København K
0045 33 14 40 02

Mandrup-Poulsen Tapeter
Boulevarden 5
9000 Ålborg
0045 96 25 85 05
www.mixogmatch.dk

PANG Christianshavn
Sankt Annæ gade 31
1416 København K
0045 32 96 68 00

Plint A/S
Lindegården
5466 Asperup
0045 87 85 00 00
www.plint.dk

FRANCE
Antoine et Lili
95 quai de Valmy
75010 Paris
0033 140373486
www.antoineetlili.com

Bonton
5 boulevard Filles du
Calvaire
75003 Paris
0033 142723469
www.bonton.fr

Le Petit Souk
13 rue de Paris
59000 Lille
0033 3 2074 2839
www.sabre.fr

GERMANY
Himmelblau
Nymphenburger Str. 179
80634 München
0049 89 162 308

Kontrast GmbH
Hanauer Landstrasse 297
60314 Frankfurt am Main
0049 69 90 439 30
www.kontrastmoebel.de

Libelle
Kaiserallee 53
73133 Karlsruhe
0049 721 29973

Max.Leben
Untermarkt 17
82515 Wolfratshausen
0049 8178 609282

Takatomo
Jülicher Straße 24a
50674 Köln
0049 221 6916042
www.takatomo.de

Tribeca
An den Quellen 1
65183 Wiesbaden
0049 611 370219

IRELAND
Avoca
Rathcoole , Fitzmaurice
Road
Co Dublin
00353 12571800
www.avoca.ie

Avoca
11-13 Suffolk Street
Co Dublin 2
00353 12571800
www.avoca.ie

Avoca
Molls Gap
Ring of Kerry
Kenmare
Co. Kerry
00353 12571800
www.avoca.ie

Brown Thomas Store
Avoca level 2
18-21 Patrick Street
Co Cork
00353 12571800
www.avoca.ie

NORTHERN IRELAND
Avoca Belfast
41 Arthur Street
Belfast BT1 4GB
44 28 90 279 950
www.avoca.ie

ISRAEL
Sofi
45/3 Allenby St
63325 Tel-Aviv
00972 35162077

ITALY
Grassagallina Snc
Piazza del Popolo 23a
40017 San Giovanni in
Persicet
0039 51827079
www.grassagallina.com

JAPAN
Mum's Little Things
1-21-4 Hamamatsucho
4F Minato Bldg
105-0013 Minato-ku
Tokyo
0081 3 5425 2715

MEXICO
Casa Palacio
Centro Comercial Antara
Ejercitio Nacional 843-B
11520 Mexico D.F
0052 5.59991E+11
www.casapalacio.com.mx

THE NETHERLANDS
Lant van Texsel
Waalderstraat 23
1791 EB Den Burg
0031 222322031
www.winkeloptexel.nl

Nijhof
Minervaweg 3
3741 GR Baarn
0031 35 5486192
www.nijhofbaarn.nl

Zinin
Burg. Reigerstraat 11
3581 KJ Utrecht
0031 302518178
www.zininshop.nl

NEW ZEALAND
Allium Interiors
11 Teed Street
Newmarket
1023 Auckland
0064 95244242
www.alliuminteriors.co.nz

Emilie
166 Marua Road
Ellerslie, Auckland
0064 95719375

Iko Iko
118 Cuba Street
Te Aro
6011 Wellington
0064 43850977
www.ikoiko.co.nz

Iko Iko
195 Karangahape Road
Newton, 1011 Auckland
0064 93580220
www.ikoiko.co.nz

NORWAY
Britts Boutique
Heiloveien 4
9015 Tromsø
0047 77607195

Grønn
Lilleakerveien 31
0283 Oslo
0047 22519700

Hakallegården
Hakallestranda
6149 Åram, Vanylven
0047 7001588
www.alpakka.no

Libertine A/S
Storgata 42
2609 Lillehammer
0047 97658313

Lunehjem
Øvre Langgatan 42
3110 Tønsberg
0047 47246976
www.lunehjem.no

Ting Oslo
Akersgata
18 0158 Oslo
0047 22424242
www.tingbutikken.no

SINGAPORE

The Children's Showcase
501 Bukit Timah Road
#02-31/33 Cluny Court
259760 Singapore
0065 64747440

SPAIN

Suit Beibi
Benet Mateu, 52
8034 Barcelona
0034 609446688
www.suitbeibi.com

SWEDEN

Artiklar
Fleminggatan 65
112 32 Stockholm
0046 8 652 93 35

Inreda
Tryffelslingan 12
181 57 Lidingö
0046 8 446 05 45

Ombonat
Sundsesplanaden 3
82430 Hudiksvall
0046 650 14959

Ordbrukaren/Lukket
Broarne Sätra Brunn
Lövåsen 142
733 95 Sala
0046 224 547 26

HONG KONG

Attic Lifestyle
53 Wong Chuk Road Unit 4,
12th Floor
Hong Kong
www.attic-lifestyle.com

Sousi
9 Gough Street
Hong Kong
00852 25442255

Tiny Footprints
10/F 1 Duddell Street
Hong Kong
0085 269084618
www.tinyfootprints.com

UNITED KINGDOM

Aimé
32 Ledbury Road
London W11 2AB
0044 2072217070
www.aimelondon.com

Burford Garden Company
Shilton Road
Burford OX18 4PA
0044 1993823117
www.bgc.co.uk

Eden Rose
7 Burkes Court
Burkes Road
Beaconsfield HP9 1NZ
0044 1494678779
www.edensroseboutique.
com

Fig 1
51 St Lukes Road
Bristol BS3 4RX
0044 1173308167
www.fig1.co.uk

Fuego
5a Coombe Street
Lyme Regis DT7 3PY
Dorset
0044 1297443933
www.fuegoshop.co.uk

Gazebo
74 High Street
Totnes TQ9 5SN
0044 1803863679
www.whatalovelyshop.
co.uk

Indian Summer
624c Fulham Road
Parsons Green
London SW6 5RS
0044 2077318234
www.indiansummershop.
com

Kidsen
111 Chamberlayne Road
London NW10 3NS
0044 2089697566
www.kidsen.co.uk

Liberty London
Regent Street
London W1B 5AH
0044 207734 1234
www.liberty.co.uk

Olive loves Alfie
84 Stoke Newington
Church Street
London N16 0AP
0044 2072414212
www.olivelovesalfie.co.uk

Oiiver Bonas
129 Kensington High
Street
London W8 6SU
0044 2079374686
www.oliverbonas.com

The Orchid House
15 Lake Road
Keswick CA12 5BS
0044 1768772875
www.theorchidhouse.net

Ottie and the Bea
12 Old Dover Road
Blackheath
London SE3 7BT
0044 2084655318
www.ottieandthebea.co.uk

Nettle Green
0044 8456522678
www.nettlegreen.co.uk

Pinks & Green
0044 7772324624
www.pinksandgreen.co.uk

Rockett St George
0044 1444253391
www.rockettstgeorge.
co.uk

Shirleyz
Heathlands Rd, Unit 2
Holme Grange Craft Village
Wokingham RG40 3AW
0044 1183277022
www.shirleyz.com

Sisters Guild
0044 137371988
www.sistersguild.co.uk

Sixtyseven
67 Dyke Road
Brighton BN1 3JE
0044 1273735314
www.shopsixtyseven.
co.uk

**Tomlinsons & The Dulwich
Trade**
11 Croxted Road
London SE21 8SZ
0044 20 87613457
www.rigbyandmac.com

Wickle
24 High Street
Lewes BN7 2LU
0044 1273487969
www.wickle.co.uk

UNITED STATES

ABC Carpet & Home
888 & 881 Broadway
New York
New York 10003
212 473 3000
www.abchome.com

ABC Carpet & Home
777 South Congress
Avenue
Delray Beach
Florida 33445
561 279 7777
www.abchome.com

**The Famous
Concord Shop**
13 Walden Street
Concord
Massachusetts 01742
978 371 2286
www.concordshop.com

Genius Outfitters
346 Lewers Street
Honolulu
Hawaii 96815
808 922 2822
www.geniusoutfitters.com

Harts N Crafts
1125 S. 8th Street
Waco
Texas 76706
254 754 3350
www.hartsncrafts.com

Huset
1316 1/2 Abbot Kinney
Boulevard
Venice
California 90291
424 268 4213
www.huset-shop.com

Lulu London
815 464 2974
www.shopsweetlulu.com

Modern Dane
2169 Mabey Drive
Salt Lake City
Utah 84109
801 901 0515

Nicerworld
415 335 4200
www.nicerworld.com

Rosie True San Marco
1949 San Marco Boulevard
Jacksonville
Florida 32207
904 396 7463
www.rosietrue.com

Rosie True The Beaches
2400-104 South Third
Street
Jacksonville Beach
Florida 32250
904 247 8464
www.rosietrue.com

So Perfect Eats
278 Fillmore Street
Denver
Colorado 80206
917 679 7563
www.soperfecteats.com

Whisk
231 Bedford Avenue
Brooklyn
New York 11211
718 218 7230
www.whisknyc.com

Whisk
933 Broadway
New York
New York 10010
212 477 8680
www.whisknyc.com

Yolk
1626 Silverlake Boulevard
Los Angeles
California 90026
323 660 4315
www.shopyolk.com

This book was bought at:

ACKNOWLEDGMENTS

A heartfelt thank you to Holly Becker—you came to my old house and styled some fabulous pictures for your book *Decorate*, and through these I got the contact to the publisher Jacqui Small and the lovely people there. I am not sure how to really thank you enough for this—in the good old Danish tradition we are not very strong on giving compliments. But I feel really privileged and happy that we have met—you are a great inspiration, and I look forward to sharing a long road ahead with you.

Sian Parkhouse—thank you for your quiet patience and your talent for keeping it simple at all times. Thanks to Sarah Rock for a great layout. To Jacqui Small and Jo Copestick—for the lovely lunches from Ottolenghi. I might need to come back.

It's been a fun and joyous ride and I want to send lots of warm thanks to the wonderful people who opened their homes to us. Thank you for sharing bits of your personal everyday-magic space. It has been a privilege.

Special thanks to my old friend and stylist Birgitte Møller Nielsen for invaluable styling help, and to Mitzi Nielsen for eagle eyes and great help in the writing process. What a great team we all make. Thank you to my family and the rest of my sweet colleagues at RICE for your patience while I have been busy with the writing.

All photographs were taken by Joachim Wichmann and John Bendtsen from wichmann+bendsten photography except the following:

Lykke Foged: p46, p47, and p111 bottom

Therese Hagstedt: pp96, p107, p151, and p161

Kaspar Kamuk: p51 top row 1, p52 far right, p67 top row 2, 3 and 4 and bottom row 3 and 4; p103 top row 5 and bottom row 1, 2, 3, 4 and 5, p108 right, p109, p110, p114 left, p146 left, p154, p168, p169 bottom row 1, p189 bottom row 4, and p192

Brigitte Kroone: p9 top left, p17, p28 bottom, p41 top row 3 and bottom row 1 and 3, p74 bottom, p84, p90 bottom right, p111 top left, p112, p135 top row 1, p136 bottom right, p150, p160 top left, and p169 top row 4

31901052020775